CONTENTS

Preface
Introduction: Definitions and Scope

- *Billionaires by Race and Ethnicity*
- *Kleptocracy: Old and New Definitions*

Analysis 1: Warren Buffett: "Oracle of Omaha" or River City Racist?

Preface
Introduction
The Buffett Family History: Some Selected Notes

- *Doris Buffett: Some Personal Notes*
- *Doris Buffett and the Sunshine Lady Foundation*

Warren Buffett: A Biographical Critique
Warren Buffett: Exploitation of Minorities

- *Clayton Homes in Gallup, New Mexico: Native Americans*
- *75 North in North Omaha, Nebraska*

Conclusion: The Cover-ups Will Continue ...

Analysis 2 - Straight Outta Africa: Bill Gates' "Mandela Lecture," His Vision, His Values Plans -- A Look at Modern Post-Colonial Thinking

Introduction
Contextual Appraisal: White Folks and Africa

- **Post-Colonial Thinking: Analysis**

Contextual Appraisal: White Folks and Africa
As Things Change, So They Remain the Same
Bill Gates and the Mandela Lecture: Critique and Commentary
Conclusion
References

Conclusion
References

Preface

Like Bill Gates, Warren Buffett spent a great deal of time in 2016 claiming to be giving away his money to the poor. While he's making all these grandiose claims to the national public and his racist stakeholders, his daughter is cannibalistically chewing up Omaha's black community, buying land and housing and exploiting the poor. The same thing that Warren is doing in various parts of the country.

In 1996 I applied for a grant to the Buffett Foundation, based in Omaha, less than five miles from the largest Black community in the state. His Executive Director of the Foundation, Allen Greenberg, wrote me a letter in March of 1996 which said, *"This is in response to your letter requesting a grant from the Buffett*

Foundation. I am sorry but the Foundation's grant making is limited to projects concerning world population needs. This does not include the kind of work your group is proposing to undertake."

And I knew that – I just wanted it in writing.

You see, my organizations are about life and liberation of black people – not about population control, which is what that Jew just described. Buffett, like others before him including Thomas Malthus and Aldous Huxley, author of *Brave New World*, are concerned that poor people are going to overpopulate the world and there won't be anything left for peckerwoods. So when they talk about "world population needs," they are talking about population CONTROL, birth CONTROL and wiping out as many niggas as possible. There is an organization based on Washington, DC called "Zero Population Growth" that does the same shit, but also works to increase the numbers of peckerwoods in the world.

And Buffett has also been involved in controlling the population on the other end: by selling cigarettes and giving people cancer. During the 1987 Nabisco takeover he even admitted that he loves investing in the cigarette industry because it only costs a penny to make, you can sell it for a dollar and – it's addictive. Ain't that a bitch? This is the same guy that Omaha's media paints as some kind of "oracle" when, as I will show, he's just another white man with a hidden racist agenda.

And then there's Bill Gates, much more innocent looking, skinnier and more stable in terms of family life. But a kleptocrat is a kleptocrat because of what they DO, not what they SAY because they'll say anything.

Let me confess to a bias from the get-go. As a scholar and historian, I do not trust white people. No matter how well-meaning they claim to be, how many donations they make to black causes, no matter how many black girlfriends or pals they have, their history is enough to show me that, as the African proverb teaches us, "It is a wise warrior who moves with caution and discretion when an enemy throws bouquets in his direction."

I like Bill and Linda Gates and their move to give away a lot of their massive fortune. But again, history tells me not to trust a white man who wants to "give" something to black people. Karenga (1967) wrote long ago that, "The white man has three ways of controlling Blacks: the missionary, the mercenary and the military." I recall well the words of the late Stokely Carmichael (Kwame Ture) who said in October of 1966 in front of a throng of students at UC-Berkeley:

> That we're not talking about a policy or aid or sending Peace Corps
> people in to teach people how to read and write and build houses
> while we steal their raw materials from them. Is that what we're

> talking about? 'Cause that's all we do. What underdeveloped countries needs -- information on how to become industrialized, so they can keep their raw materials where they have it, produce them and sell it to this country for the price it's supposed to pay; not that we produce it and sell it back to them for a profit and keep sending our modern day missionaries in, calling them the sons of Kennedy. And that if the youth are going to participate in that program, how do you raise those questions where you begin to control that Peace Corps program? How do you begin to raise them?

That was in 1966 – just over half a century ago. In my view I believe this is what Bill Gates and those other "do-gooder" white philanthropists are up to. I have written this brief paper to support this belief.

Warrant Buffett and Bill Gates are both thoroughgoing capitalists, and they want to keep it that way. What they do behind closed doors is not known to much of the public, but we do know that the majority of their supporters and shareholders are as white as they are. Their sporadic doling out of charity and grants in no way overrides the dirt that they have done to nations and communities of color, Gates perhaps less so than Buffett. But that means nothing: am I going to cut Frank James slack because he killed fewer people than Jesse James? Of course not.

This is not a comprehensive examination. It is an analysis to provide a different look at kleptocracy in action and how the "new wave kleptocrats" shroud their greed and racism in acts of what could be called "pseudo-benevolence." This book is a seed that I hope to plant to get you, the readers, to do more research, be more critical of men like these. They are sly, slick and wicked. As the lyrics from the 1971 song by the Undisputed Truth warned us,

> Smiling faces sometimes
> Pretend to be your friend
> Smiling faces show no traces
> Of the evil that lurks within …
>
> … Beware, beware of the handshake
> That hides the snake
> I'm telling you beware
> Beware of the pat on the back
> It just might hold you back

Warren Buffett and Bill Gates may appear to be physically dissimilar. But they are cut from the same cloth. A billionaire will tell you in most cases that they are "self-made." But that's what the plantation owners in the Deep South claimed too when they beat and killed our ancestors and worked them from "can't see in the morning until can't see at night." As those slavemasters built an empire on the backs of African people they were at the same time boasting about how all that wealth in the cotton economy was a product of hard work – by whites.

Much of the information on kleptocracy deals with government officials who steal from the masses of people. I beg to differ. The ACT of kleptocracy is closely related to the root word which means "thief" – as in "kleptomaniac." So it is the theft that is of importance, not the source of the theft. If a man has a corporation and uses the profits to amass more money by exploiting the public and taking land and resources as a result, that man is a "kleptocrat." I will provide examples and brief case studies elsewhere in this book.

In today's technocratic and social media-dominated society stand two men who are racial relatives of those slavemasters. One uses business acumen and investment strategies to maintain his version of kleptocracy while the other uses computer technology to maintain his empire. Study will the backgrounds and words of each man that I have shared with you in this book because I didn't do all this research for my health. I did it to rip the veil off of the lie that these two billionaires are "good old guys" and that because they now want to give away a portion of their wealth that they are somehow absolved of what they've done to black people all over the world. People may object to my views on both Buffett and Gates.

All I can say in response is, *"Objection overruled!"*

Introduction: Definition and Scope

I have always said and believed that white people are always more committed to their whiteness than they are to any "ism." So when I heard descriptions of whites who believed in communism, or democratic socialism or any kind of ideology, I realized that it was the white race first, and the ideology a distant second. This applies both Buffett and Gates.

Billionaires by Race and Ethnicity

Kleptocrats are about greed and money is the key. The two men in this book claim to be "self-made billionaires" (as do a large percentage of these rich guys), but the facts point to a major personality trait: the quest for power and control.

Most of the world's billionaires are white, with Asians coming in a close second. In the entire world, only six billionaires are Black. So as one source informs us, "even though blacks are 15% of the World's population, they are only 0.42% of the World's richest. Thus their representation among the super rich is only 2.8% of their population share. White (Gentiles) are 16% of the World's population, but 41.65% of the World's billionaires, thus their representation among the super rich is 260% of their population share. Jews are only 0.2% of the World's population, but 17.46% of the World's richest. Thus their representation is 8,730% of their population share. (World Atlas, 2018)

> There are more billionaires than ever and they are richer than ever too. That's according to Forbes' annual ranking of the world's billionaires, published Tuesday. There are a record 2,208 billionaires in the world, up from 2,043 in 2017, according to Forbes. And the average wealth of the billionaires is $4.1 billion, a record high. Taken together, the billionaires of the world are worth $9.1 trillion, up from $7.7 trillion last year, Forbes reports … Many of the top spots on the list are held by self-made entrepreneurs. (Clifford, 2018).

Show me a billionaire and I'll show you a white nationalist. Don't be fooled by the recent attempts by politicians and the media to point to groups like the Ku Klux Klan and the Nazi Party and dub them white nationalists – as if the white majority in America is not. They are ALL white nationalists and if you don't believe it, look at their behavior during President's Day and the Fourth of July – paying homage to a nation that they KNOW murdered off tens of thousands of First Nation people. That's white nationalism.

A billionaire has to be a kleptocrat (definitions forthcoming) because if you are a white nationalist, your purpose is to "build whiteness." That is how racism and discrimination based on race have persisted over centuries. These white people build on their values and beliefs. That is why their language, as it was in their native Europe, continues to associate all that is negative, dirty and inferior with "blackness" or "darkness," and all that is great, glorious and clean with "whiteness."

With preliminary information on billionaires having been offered, let us now move to a better understanding of "kleptocracy" and what it means.

<u>Kleptocracy: Old and New Definitions</u>

As I usually do when I seek operational definitions, I consult five to six dictionaries for the most thorough definition. When it comes to describing a "kleptocracy," I found it to be "A political system ruled by a leader who misuses his power and country resources", and a "kleptocrat" is obviously the person who who engineers these thefts. I would add that the engineering can be done either directly or indirectly.

So then, when these leaders make themselves powerful by stealing from the rest of the people, then it is called as kleptocracy. More profoundly, let's see what the World Atlas has to say about the term and the system:

> Kleptocracy is a term with negative connotations, used to define a form of leadership **where senior government officials use their authority to embezzle public funds for self-gain and to solidify their political prominence.** Kleptocracy is often practiced under autocratic governments where external supervision is mostly non-existent, and therefore the disbursement and use of public funds are dictated by the nation's leadership. **These corrupt government officials use the funds meant for the development of the country, for personal gain.** (World Atlas, 2018 – emphasis added)

Again, if you have a corporate entity that is using funds meant for development and you use that money for personal gain, what difference does it make it you're a "governmental entity" or not? A kleptocrat is a thief and that is what is important. The two white men I deal with in this book are not politicos (at least not directly), but they have a shared political belief: the belief in white nationalism and the token exploitation of black people to push their own causes. That is the mentality of a slavemaster, or a dominative racist. Stripped of the smiles and the elderly gait, Buffett and Gates are white nationalists who use capitalism to amass wealth. It is not what they say, it is what they DO that should be analyzed.

Moving on to differentiate between the denotative definition of the kleptocracy and my definition, which is rooted in the world of reality and the impact of the greed that today's examples have on the masses of people:

> There are numerous examples of such governments around the world, where the nation's leadership has accumulated mind-boggling amounts of wealth at the expense of the majority of the citizens. **Kleptocracies are closely associated with military juntas, oligarchies, dictatorships, and other types of nepotism or autocratic regimes, where external oversight is nonexistent or is impossible.** The absence of monitoring could be worsened by the corrupt officials who control the supply and means of distribution of public funds. **Kleptocratic leaders treat the county's resources as personal items and spend them on luxuries and extravagance, and many of them transfer the country's funds to**

> **secret accounts in foreign countries.** (World Atlas, 2018 – emphasis added)

Kleptocracies MAY be associated with military juntas but I charge that this doesn't have to be the case. I recall a slogan by a cultural nationalist from the '60s who once wrote that, "The white man has three ways of controlling blacks: gift, gun and ideological game." Transposing that idea to an extent, the would be kleptocrat doesn't just have to rely on "the gun." He can use "gifts and ideological game." That is what Gates has done with Microsoft, is it not? That is what Buffett has done with Berkshire-Hathaway, is it not? The former a computer giant that claims to want to serve the world and the latter a giant conglomerate that innocently makes money in a number of areas. They need not have the backing of violence when both men have mastered the art and science of "mis-direction." And both men have the backing of the national and international media.

According to the World Atlas,

> **Russia is often pointed out as an example of a modern kleptocracy, and the nation's current president, Vladimir Putin is described as the "true definition of a kleptocratic leader."** While the astronomical rise of Vladimir Putin to the Russian political summit was fueled by promises of removing all oligarchies in the country, the president would later take up kleptocratic tendencies on attaining the presidency and began amassing wealth. In Putin's regime, an estimated 35% of the country's wealth is controlled by 110 people.(World Atlas, 2018 – emphasis added)

I have long said that if you stand a Russian next to an American, you can't tell the difference. Both are white, and that is why they might insult one another but they won't fight because it's a "family affair." White nationalism trumps any "tribal differences" that may exist. Putin's kleptocracy is really not much different from American Democracy when you look at the fact that in the United States, you have a very similar situation when you account for race:

> Just prior to President Obama's 2014 State of the Union Address, media … reported that **the top wealthiest 1% possess 40% of the nation's wealth; the bottom 80% own 7%;** similarly, but later, the media reported, the **"richest 1 percent in the United States now own more additional income than the bottom 90 percent"** (Wikipedia, 2018 – emphasis added)

Don't haggle over the percentages because that doesn't matter. It is akin to being "a little bit pregnant." Either you are a kleptocrat or you're not. America may be in the early stages of what might be called "full blown kleptocracy," but it's coming, believe me. Greed begats more greed. Even as I write these words, look at the way that the current President, Donald J. Trump, is transforming America into a veritable kleptocracy. More on this elsewhere in this book.

The World Atlas and others look at all of the African countries that steal from their people and are kleptocratic leaders. So typical, but here is what is said, in part":

> … Former Zaire (present-day Democratic Republic of Congo) leader, President Mobutu Sese Seko was among the most corrupt leaders of the 20th century. Under Mobutu's leadership, Zaire's economy had all but collapsed and experienced unprecedented hyperinflation. Zimbabwe's longest-serving head of state, former president Robert Mugabe was a well-known kleptocrat … Another well-known kleptocrat in modern Africa is Uganda's President Yoweri Museveni. (World Atlas, 2018)

It's called "deflection." Even as President Trump is literally taking over the American system and using American taxpayers' money to buttress his hotel empire, these people are pointing to Africa, the same continent that they (white Americans) sought to pillage for centuries. And as this book shows, at least in part, even Bill Gates sees the potential in Africa and before you send in the military and the mercenaries you first send in the missionaries. In this case it's the "Microsoft Holy book." More on that later.

Speaking of Trump, check out the following:

> The United States has often been portrayed as the model of true democracy, but surprisingly the American government has in recent years been labeled as a kleptocracy. **President Donald Trump has been a polarizing figure in American politics, with his leadership style endearing him to some and earning him critics in equal measure.** However, the fact remains that President Trump shares characteristics of other well-known kleptocratic leaders, **with nepotism being manifested in the making of significant appointments during his presidency**. (World Atlas, 2018 – emphasis added)

America is no model of true democracy. The word democracy comes from the Greek word that translates to mean "rule by the people." America has never been ruled by the people. America has long been dominated and directed by elites: white men, white landlowners and white farmer types. Women and people of color were not allowed – akin to what takes place in most kleptocracies where one group is in power and calls the shots for all the rest.

In my book *Donald Trump as White Male Prototype*, I make it clear that he is the rule, not the exception. But his gradual leaning toward creating a kleptocracy has brought him closer than all of the others, including elitist slaveholders like Washington, Adams and Jefferson.

> The US constitution makes it impossible for President Trump to become a true kleptocrat, capable of appointing his wife as Vice President. However, such kleptocratic characteristics like nepotism are not exclusive to the Trump administration. **President John F Kennedy infamously appointed his brother, Robert as the nation's attorney general, a move that was met with bitter criticism.** (World Atlas, 2018 – emphasis added)

So bits and pieces of the kleptocratic tendency have existed and as stated, the current president of the United States is dragging the nation even closer.

At the same time we cannot help but add that just as military coups and takeovers have led to kleptocracies in other parts of the world, so have major drug cartels and the money generated.

The World Atlas informs us that, "Narcokleptocracy, also known as narco-states or narco-economies, are nations where drug money has compromised the integrity of the government through the bribing of senior government officials. Using their bottomless accounts drug barons force the government to allow the illegal drug trade to be conducted within the country. Some countries that have been defined as narco-economies include Guinea-Bissau, Panama, Tajikistan, and Venezuela. Narco-economies share many characteristics of kleptocracies, since very few individuals holding influential positions in government, control most of the country's wealth and leaving the majority to languish in poverty. (World Atlas, 2018).

The fact is, America is what I would call a "quasi-narcokleptocracy." What I mean is that the drugs aren't of the street variety – not crack cocaine, methamphetamine, LSD, pills. The "peddlers" and dealers aren't named Guerrero or Williams or Chung. The major "dealers" in America go by the name Walgreen's, Osco, CVS, Rite-Aid and of course, Wal-Mart. These are the major drug outlets and the "dealers" are every single doctor with a prescription pad. These drug dealers are controlled by the FDA – the Food and Drug Administration – but it is slowly but surely getting out of control with the advent of major pharmaceutical companies like Pfizer, GlaxoSmithKlein, Novartis, Eli Lilly, Johnson & Johnson, and Merck & Company – to name but a few. Their profits are in the hundreds of millions per year.

You have your definition of narcokleptocracy and I have mine. But the question to ask is "What are the effects of kleptocracy of any kind"? According to the World Atlas,

> The funds misappropriated by kleptocratic regimes are meant for the provision of essential social services such as in health, education, food, and water. Therefore, the majority of the citizenry in such countries lives in deplorable conditions and lack basic amenities. **Only a few individuals in senior government positions and their associates benefit from kleptocracies often through dealing with corrupt activities.** (World Atlas, 2018 – emphasis added)

Of course the previous definition is tempered by the type of country we are talking about. Many of these countries have the same "types" and "groups" of people but the fact still remains that there are going to be "haves" and "have nots." So the insinuation that the services being deprived are "above board" before the grab by the government is more than likely a false proposition. It is my view that kleptocracies rise because of the attitudes, values and orientations of the people who are greedy and shrewd enough to manipulate the system to suit them. There is no purity one day and the next day there's a takeover. No, it is gradual and it is planned. Some are the result of military takeovers and others are not. But all are the product of greed.

Therefore,

> Kleptocracies often have a terrible reputation in the international scene, and hence lack foreign investments and therefore weaken the cross-border trade and the domestic market. **Kleptocratic leaders misuse funds obtained from tax payments and engage in money laundering, which adversely affects the quality of life of the citizens in the whole country.** (World Atlas, 2018 – emphasis added)

What was just described is the beginning of what is taking place in America under current President Donald Trump. This is part of the reason why I chose the name "new kleptocrats." The goals and tendencies are still the same, but the tactics and process used to steal and horde away from the masses may have differed because of an alert news media and social media in general. But the goal, the greed and the grotesque gooniness – all of which Trump surely possesses – are right there in the mix.

The "new kleptocrats" really don't need military takeovers to steal from the masses. They can do so through policy, legislation and laws all aimed at "taking." This is already taking place in a number of local communities around the nation with cities and counties using "Eminent Domain" and various code enforcement strategies to take and relocate certain populations. And by "certain populations" I mean Blacks, Latinos, First Nation people and refugees. They can use fake evacuations, natural disasters as a cover for taking over entire areas and the media to circulate lies about gas leaks, electrical problems, prospective black outs and coming soon: the zombie apocalypse. A takeover is a takeover regardless of how it is accomplished.

Indeed, Trump is setting the stage by surrounding himself with family members, equally scurrilous people and those who are loyal to him and blind to his on-going atrocities. White people are slow on the uptake when it comes to seeing criminal intent when it is committed by their own people because they are too busy staring at what's going on in the ghetto, the barrio and on the reservation. But people like Warren Buffett and Bill Gates, smiling away, will introduce a new form of kleptocracy, akin to former President Richard Nixon's weird concept of "benign neglect."

Analysis I –
Warren Buffett: "Oracle of Omaha" or River City Racist?

The Buffett Family History: Selective Information

When I first heard about Warren Buffett being the richest man in the world, and when I learned he was from Omaha, Nebraska, I realized that this man, on some level, was a racist. There were no articles about it because people with that kind of money can control the media. In fact, Buffett owns the Omaha World Herald, DirecTV, 21st Century Fox and owns newspapers all over the nation, including states like Iowa, New Jersey, Oklahoma, Virginia, North and South Carolina, Alabama, Florida, and Texas. And as Mao taught, "He who controls images controls minds, and he who controls minds has little, if anything, to worry about from bodies."

Warren Buffett has been in Omaha all of his life. He has traveled all over the world and has an international reputation for his wealth. What people never mention is that in the city of his residence, there is a black community, some 8-square miles in circumference, that is one of the poorest in the nation. In fact, it ranks number one in the nation in black child poverty and also number one in black-on-black youth homicide. It is an area where a huge percentage of its residence survive on public aid. Buffett does nothing but invade that community, build structures that those residents cannot afford, construct child care centers that accept only Title XX clients and bleeds the area for his own purposes. This will all be documented in this book.

The Buffett's all share what I call "a greediness gene" when it comes to their so-called philanthropy. Doris doles out chump change from her mansion in Boston and Warren unrepentantly goes after any "target market" that is low-income, minority and therefore vulnerable to any real estate sales pitch that his lackeys might launch. Following is information that local media refuse to touch.

Doris Buffett: Some Personal Notes

His sister Doris was quite a looker during her younger years. But other than that, she must have been somewhat bereft of common sense as she was married and divorced four times. And yet Warren saw fit to put her in charge of the Sunshine Lady Foundation located in Boston, where it is her job to do nothing more than give away money. More on that later.

Check out Doris' track record:

> Doris Buffett, who has been married four times and has three children, has paid for used cars, dentures, winter boots, tooth extractions, hearing aids, children's clothing, furnaces, funerals, and tombstones. The money does not go directly to individuals; instead, Buffett and her volunteers buy the requested items and have them delivered, or send payments to mortgage companies, utilities, and other creditors. . (Pfeiffer, 2016).

First things first.

Doris Buffett has been married four times and has three children. Is she paying child support? Were the guys wealthy or broke and taking advantage of her name and status? Why didn't the marriages last and more importantly, why does this article just skip and skim over these details as if being married four times is not a sign of something being "wrong" in a number of ways? Maybe it has to do with her health, a factor that is implied in the following excerpt:

> "You are thrilled when you can answer somebody's prayers," said Buffett, who moved to Boston in October to be closer to her doctors; she is being treated for several medical issues. . (Pfeiffer, 2016).

How is she going to answer someone's prayers when she can't even take care of herself? She needs to save those "prayers" for whatever is ailing her! Furthermore, if the average amount of the money she gives out is only $4,800 as is stated elsewhere in this book, then that sure is a skimpy-ass prayer!

This doesn't sound much like a foundation – the way it is described it seems more like a "poor house" or some kind of nonprofit referral agency. Check it out:

> The volume of incoming letters, many of which arrive handwritten on loose-leaf paper, fluctuates. It surges whenever Warren or Doris Buffett makes a media appearance, as well as after natural disasters and economic downturns, like the mortgage collapse. The Buffetts estimate they make at least 250 gifts each year totaling about $1.2 million, although some years the annual total has exceeded $2 million. . (Pfeiffer, 2016).

Chump change! They give it out and then they write it off – the way most of these rich white people tend to do. A funky 250 "gifts" a year? That's all? That's about one gift a day. Now when compared and contrasted with all the people who are in dire straits, all the disasters and such, the mounts and the frequency of the gifts, when you consider all the money the Buffetts have, is chump change!

And here's how it works:

> The money is funneled through Doris Buffett's Sunshine Lady Foundation, which she created with an inheritance in 1996 and which also receives funding requests from strangers. Warren Buffett transfers Berkshire Hathaway stock — now worth more than $221,000 for each class A share — to replenish the fund when it gets low. . (Pfeiffer, 2016).

In January of 2017 HBO began airing a so-called "documentary" called "Becoming Warren Buffett." The one-sided story made him sound like some kind of Horatio Algier story when, in reality, what I am writing in this paper are realities that show Buffett as he is from the eyes of the people who live in the same city and who realize the segregated reality of Buffett's life, a reality that he did not lift a single finger to address.

The same can be said for his sister, Dorothy. They are poverty pimps, as another section of this book clearly shows, and these are realities that the media avoids because they are the voice of the status quo. For instance, Pfeiffer (2016) thinks that the following description of Doris Buffett and her foundation is flattering:

> Writing checks from someone else's checkbook might sound like a
> fantasy job, but it's rigorous work on Doris Buffett's watch.
> Volunteers do background checks on letter writers, including
> research on their income, assets, and debts. They contact
> references, which grant applicants are required to supply. .
> (Pfeiffer, 2016)

How is writing a check from someone else's checkbook a "fantasy job" or, for that matter, even "rigorous work." When the donations you give are tax deductible, all you are is a poverty pimp. You sit around pontificating about how you "help the poor" when in reality, all you are doing is helping yourself TO the poor. Just like Warren does with his construction programs that are documented in this book. Doris is no different, just on a more "social service" type level.

Continuing:

> Sometimes, rather than provide money, the volunteers teach letter
> writers how to budget and connect them to government services or
> nonprofit groups that can lend assistance. They must also be on the
> alert for scam artists, such as people who write numerous letters
> from the same address using different names. And they have to
> learn to gently say no. . (Pfeiffer, 2016).

This is a welfare agency, not a foundation. This woman is sitting on all this money and yet they appear to have what I call a "poverty vetting process." They want to provide options to what the people came for – money! They want to teach them to write "leech letters" on how they can get money *elsewhere*. So the "bad guys," the scam artists, are the ones who write letters from the same address? After reading about the dirt that her brother Warren has pulled on poor people, these Buffetts have a lot of gall to even utter the word "scam." And that also includes Doris.

What is paternalistic racism? In this case it would be "maternalistic" racism, but it is basically the same. It is defined as, "This implies that the majority race in one country or setting has the right to rule over the minority race for its own good (Halstead 1988). Paternalistic racism is particularly related to Blacks or African Americans and Whites in the United States. It implies that White people have the right to interfere with the lives of Black people for their own good. Furthermore, the majority race has the right to define what is good for the minority race …" (Hall, 2017). This is how Warren, Doris and Warren's daughter Susie treat people of color, having been well trained by practicing on the backward negroes of Omaha.

Continuing, a flunky for the rich man's "mommy dearest" explains,

> "Sometimes it's tough love," said Campbell, who now works for Doris Buffett. "If you're going to lose your house because no way with your income could you possibly support a mortgage like that, we might say, 'You have to face reality and find something you can afford.' . . . It can be very heartbreaking." . (Pfeiffer, 2016).

What about organizational donations? How about groups that are out in the streets working to combat drug abuse, teen pregnancy, HIV/AIDS and such? What if someone comes forward with an idea that deals with the psychological problems of white racism? Do you think any of these conservative hacks would ever give up a donation for such a cause? Of course not.

Now pay close attention to the contradictions and hypocrisy inherent in the following paragraph:

> Seated in the living room at the home of her grandson, Alex Buffett Rozek — who also lives in the Back Bay and manages a Boston private investment firm called Boulderado Group — Doris Buffett listed the key traits of ideal letter readers ... "They have to have a heart somewhere," said Buffett, whose nickname is Dodo and who, like her brother, grew up in Omaha. "Someone very practical. And they would not be judgmental." . (Pfeiffer, 2016).

Dodo? As in the extinct bird or "do-do" as in another word for feces? In either case, a woman with this kind of clout and family name should avoid nicknames of any kind. Just the fact that the people asking for help have to have "key traits" speaks volumes about the paternalistic racism that I allege is part and parcel of the "Buffett legacy." Doris claims, "They have to have a heart somewhere. Someone very practical. And they would not be judgmental." The fact is that she doesn't even meet these qualities! If she had a "heart," she wouldn't have to impose all these requirements to give out money that she has more than enough of. Elsewhere she claims that they don't give money away, they make "investments". Tell me, what is moral about that strategy? And as for not being judgmental, what else are the Buffetts if not some judgmental jive turkeys who sit on the throne of capitalist expansion and them pimp the living shit out of the poor?

But there are more "qualifications" for those who want to get some of that Buffett money:

> Life experience is also important, she said, because wisdom and perspective often come with age. For that reason, she usually chooses older volunteers, but Buffett said she would not rule out younger applicants because some young people are wise beyond their years. . (Pfeiffer, 2016).

If this isn't a sign of "the God complex," then what is? This white woman who has been married FOUR times is giving out advice on the value of experience? What about her experience? After the first divorce, didn't she benefit from the experience? How about after the second and third one? Something is amiss and she knows it. So to compensate for that inadequacy, she immerses herself in the control of the lives of others, people who NEED her to give them something. From that "dependency connection" she can then live vicariously through the lives of others and fulfill her maternalistic controlling behavior at the same time.

Attempting to make what Doris Buffett is doing sound like some kind of "grassroots movement," check out the following:

> Another requirement: In keeping with the homespun spirit of Buffett's operation, applicants must apply by letter, not electronically. Buffett Rozek has set up a website (www.letters.foundation) where aspiring volunteers can learn how to apply. . (Pfeiffer, 2016).

So what is she doing: handwriting analysis? Or is she so "old school" that she can't deal with the flood of emailed requests she might receive? The website she's set up is just evidence that she is doing philanthropic work and as such, might be getting a write-off of some kind. Remember her words: it's about "investments," not handouts.

Continuing:

> Warren and Doris Buffett's team philanthropy began in 2006, when he publicly announced he would give away the bulk of his wealth while he was alive, including more than $30 billion to the Bill & Melinda Gates Foundation. Buffett was immediately deluged with pleas from people whose reaction was: Warren Buffett is giving away money? I'm going to ask him for some! . (Pfeiffer, 2016).

So they call it "team philanthropy"? No wonder. Both of them are exploiting the poor and engaged in a kind of paternalism that is insulting to anyone who may be needing some money. The money is supposed to be free: but again, you read what was said earlier: they see these acts as "investments," and that is the white man's way of saying "pimping." They build educational structures for the poor, but then take only those kids whose families qualify for Title XX grants so that they (the Buffetts) can get the money back; they construct mobile home parks for the poor and then charge astronomical rents and evict people if they don't pay; and they build condos, as they are doing in Omaha, that they name after an interstate ("75 North") and put it in the poorest zip code in the state ("68111") so they can then qualify for Federal aid.

They're a "team," alright. In the same way that Frank and Jesse James were a team. Or, more appropriately, Bonnie and Clyde.

And when they actually have to deal with the poor, look at the "Oracle of Omaha's" reaction. According to Doris,

> Soon after that, "I got a phone call from Warren," Doris Buffett recalled. "He said, 'I need help! Everyone is writing in, and I've got hundreds of letters, and I can't cope with them.' " . (Pfeiffer, 2016).

"Can't cope" with the letters or simply refuses to read about other people's misery? According to the Pfeiffer article, "Speaking by phone from his office at Berkshire Hathaway's Omaha headquarters, Warren Buffett, 85, offered a similar account: "When people wrote and gave me these hard-luck stories, I just felt I had no way to feel them out as to which were legit and which weren't." The gall to talk about "legitimacy"? How can this guy sleep at night? You'll read about how he's exploiting the poor people in Mexico and as I've written, he lives less than five miles from the largest African-American ghetto in the state of Nebraska. He's no "oracle of Omaha"; he's an ofay ogre.

Moving on:

> So Doris agreed to pitch in and gathered a handful of friends and neighbors to help. "Suddenly we were getting boxes and boxes and boxes," Campbell said, "and we had a roomful of people sitting on the floor reading letters." . (Pfeiffer, 2016).

Agreed to "pitch in"? Notice that Warren didn't need any help exploiting those people of color in Mexico. Notice he didn't need any help with his stock investment portfolio. Only when it comes to helping out the truly needy does he have to call in his equally paternalistic sister and get help to hand out the money. And when they hand it out, it is basically chump change; with all kinds of rules and procedures attached. I give it a name: *philanthropic sharecropping*.

Continuing:

> Added Warren Buffett: "They were wonderful little old ladies, but they were behaving like an oiled machine, processing these requests and making sure these people weren't phonies. It was a

little cottage industry. If I'd been a film producer, I would have made a movie about it!" . (Pfeiffer, 2016).

You see? He's bragging about it and thinks its cute. This is the mentality of a prospective kleptocrat. But there are some of us with high intelligence and who know things. Do you know what a "cottage industry" is? It's a home-based business. One has to ask, was it legal? Is it documented? Is the Sunshine Foundation a non-profit that is listed? Is the house properly zoned for conducting "business"? What would be the theme of the movie? I'll tell you what it would be: how the richest man in the world pimped his sister and used a house to control the poor. That's Buffett's real legacy; all this other stuff is just fluff for the rich who are looking for a way to make some money. Evil is as evil does.

Therefore,

> The floodgates opened wider in 2010, when Warren Buffett and the Gateses — the world's richest couple — created the Giving Pledge, which asks billionaires to pledge at least half their fortunes to charity. . (Pfeiffer, 2016).

I deal with Bill and Melinda Gates in another manuscript ("Straight Outta Africa") and what Buffett was doing to the poor Indians and Mexicans and what he was doing to black people in Omaha was being done in Africa by Bill and Melinda Gates in the name of Nelson Mandela. Like takes to like, does it not. Why give half of your fortune to charity? Because those charities are the same race as Buffett and Gates, that's why! The United Way is one of the biggest poverty pimps in the history of the United States, and Warren's Buffett Susie was financing Goodwill in Omaha only to find out that the white men running it were paying themselves hundreds of thousands of dollars. It is, as Sly Stone sang back in 1971, a "Family Affair", it would seem.

So while Doris doles out the chump change ducats, Warren has his eye set on worldwide pimping. According to the Pfeifer article, "Warren Buffett said he is more inclined to large-scale philanthropy targeted at huge societal problems such as global health." No, he's more inclined to go after low-income property acquisition that he can invest in and then flip for a major profit. I've got all that documented in this book. He's also doing it in Omaha and, along with Susie, are buying up huge swaths of land all over North Omaha.

More lies are coming:

> "I like to give away money wholesale and she likes to give away money retail," he said of his sister. "I mean, she is genuinely interested in a guy who's had his pickup truck stolen or whatever it

> may be. Through no fault of their own, they've been handed a bum
> deal in their life. And I empathize with those people, but I'm not
> going to spend my days working with them. . (Pfeiffer, 2016).

How are you "giving away money" in any capacity when it's tied to a myriad of conditions? When, by your own admission, you don't believe in giving away money but you prefer to make "investments"? That is the philosophy of both Warren Buffett and his sister, Doris.

Pay close attention to Warren's own words: "Through no fault of their own, they've been handed a bum deal in their life. And I empathize with those people, but I'm not going to spend my days working with them." This is the real deal, and it is a reality that is covered up by the media that continues to refer to this man as "The Oracle of Omaha." Do you know what an oracle is? According to the Merriam-Webster Dictionary, an oracle is defined as, "a person (as a priestess of ancient Greece) through whom a deity is believed to speak." Another definition, this one from the Free Dictionary defines an "oracle" as, "A person considered to be a source of wise counsel or prophetic opinions."

In either case this "oracle of Omaha" crap places Buffett in the position of some kind of meta-human. He's either a prophet or he's in touch with a superior power. Now, hail back to that earlier statement where he says that he empathizes with the people who might have gotten a bad deal BUT, "I'm not going to spend my days working with them." So there is nothing moral about the oracle when all is said and done. He's an ice man that is about investments, not about humanity. This crap about handing out money is, at best, *conditional*.

In his own words, Warren says,

> "There's no question the money I give away does a lot of good . . .
> but Doris is giving time, and time is the scarcest commodity,"
> Warren Buffett added. "No matter who you are, you have 24 hours
> a day, and when you give time up you're giving up something
> important. So if you were keeping a scorecard in life, you'd give
> her a higher score than me.". (Pfeiffer, 2016).

I'll settle it: I'll give the both of you a grade of D-minus! And that's for the lack of character, the on-going deceptions that are being perpetrated on the public, and then for having the gall to pawn the acts of perfidy off as some form of "philanthropy." How can he prove that the money he gives away does a lot of good and if that is the case, why not give out more to those "do-gooders"?

Buffett and his family will claim to be Christians (as do most white folks). So here's something for him to consider – next time while you're reading Fortune Magazine or the Wall Street Journal, pick up the Bible, wipe the dust off it, and turn to Matthew 19:20-21 where it states, "I tell you the truth, it is hard for a rich man to enter the kingdom of heaven. Again I tell you, it is easier for a camel to go through the eye of a needle than for a rich man to enter the kingdom of God." So if he believes in the Bible, then he'd better buy some fireproof draws, because he and his family are headed in the opposite direction from Heaven. Get it?

The more I researched and read about these Buffetts (the three central characters: Warren, daughter Susie and sister Doris) the more insidious I find their acts to be. Their own words indict them. For instance, look at the following excerpt:

> Doris Buffett has firm standards for whom she will and won't help, and she trains her volunteers to maintain those rules. She won't give money, for example, to people who smoke, gamble, or accumulate debt through frivolous spending. (Pfeiffer, 2016).

So now we see the real Buffett modus operandi. You talk about philanthropy, you pay lip service to giving a damn about the poor, but when all is said and done, you admit that what you give out is about "investments" and furthermore that you have "firm standards." When you're white and rich, firm standards is a code phrase for "whites only." They might dole out a few bucks to some people of color, but you can believe that those people are more white mentally than they are anything else. That's how the Buffett's do it. Warren prances around Omaha with the likes of Michael Jordan, LeBron James and Tiger Woods, but he dare not bring them to the black community. When Hillary Clinton visited in 2016 just before the election, and then when Barack Obama came to Omaha in March of 2017 it was clearly to do one thing: pick up a check from Warren Buffett. This is how he operates, and this is his version of "philanthropy."

Meanwhile, daughter Susie gives out big cash to black men with no receipt ($150,000) and gets away with "oops, I did it again." And Doris has been married four times. It appears that all of them have issues with one-on-one relationships.

It's the God complex: rich people who are lacking in morals have the gall to impose false morals on others. You just read where Doris "won't give money, for example, to people who smoke, gamble, or accumulate debt through frivolous spending." Who in the hell is this thrice-divorced white woman to have the gall to mete out moral tips? How much does the public know about the hypocrisy that I have pointed out in this book in regard to Warren, Susie and Doris? These are people who are worse than Donald Trump. Yes, I say worse – and why? Because Trump practices what he preaches. He acts the way he says he's going to act. But people like the Buffetts are worse because they appeal to humanity and all that is moral and ethical while practicing the exact opposite!

They are capitalists, plain and simple. Doris says, "We'd be wasting our money, and we don't do that ... We're investing in you; that's the way we feel about it," and she doesn't consider such people good investments. . (Pfeiffer, 2016). Doris is a piece of work. They don't want to "waste their money," but her brother is going around claiming that he's going to give the money away. Susie is investing in Goodwill only to find out that she got bilked by some fast-talking white boy. She gives cash money to two bruthas to sponsor parties at a local high school that she claims would "cut back on crime." See how silly these people are?

What Anacharsis said about laws and the rich also applies to morality and people like the Buffetts: "Written laws are like spiders' webs, and will, like them, only entangle and hold the poor and weak, while the rich and powerful will easily break through them." And that is what the Buffetts have been doing for decades: breaking through, using various loopholes and media-backed fluff piece articles, to make it appear that they are above the fray when, in reality, they ARE the fray.

The pettiness of Buffett seems to have no bounds. Check it out:

> Buffett sometimes phones individuals herself to let them know she
> plans to give them money, and she is not hesitant to lecture those
> she believes have wayward lifestyles. That could mean advising
> them to lose weight or get credit counseling. . (Pfeiffer, 2016).

In vintage maternalistic fashion, she phones people to let them know that she doled out a few crumbs to them. Then, as is the case with the racist, she then "lectures" people who she thinks have wayward lifestyles. What about hers? Married three times and divorced three times? What was she doing that made her so undesirable to these men, made her choice of men so bad that it led to the legal breakups? Is she in any position to cast aspersions? And I've seen pictures of her: she has a lot of gall giving out weight loss advice! And what could be more insulting that an ultra-rich woman giving low-income people "credit counseling"?

It gets worse:

> "I've even offered vasectomies, and some men take me up on it,"
> she said. "If you're going to have a baby every single year"
> without a way to care for them, that's not responsible parenting,
> Buffett said. . (Pfeiffer, 2016).

Now, recall back at the beginning of this book when I wrote a personal note about having applied for a Buffett grant back in 1996. Let me reiterate the response I got from a Buffett flunky named Allen Greenberg:

> "This is in response to your letter requesting a grant from the Buffett Foundation. I am sorry but the Foundation's grant making is limited to projects concerning world population needs. This does not include the kind of work your group is proposing to undertake."

See? They've always been into some form of population control. They can do it through the vasectomies that Doris as "offered" or they can do it through "world population needs." Do you know what this means? This means the kind of population control that Dr. Paul Ehrlich was writing about in his book, *The Population Bomb*. Written in 1968 by Ehrlich and his wife, the book warned of the mass starvation of humans in the 1970s and 1980s due to overpopulation, as well as other major societal upheavals, and advocated immediate action to limit population growth. Fears of a "population explosion" were widespread in the 1950s and 1960s, but the book and its author brought the idea to an even wider audience (Robertson, 2012). In other words, the niggas are eating up all the food because they're producing children too fast.

Thomas Malthus raised similar concerns about the population in his tract, An Essay on the Principle of Population. More recently, according to my research, comes a book out of the United Kingdom by Fred Pearce (2010) called, *Peoplequake: Mass Migration, Ageing Nations and the Coming Population Crash*. Buffett doesn't help the poor any more than he does because he is a "river city racist." Like most racists he doles out small doses to foster more dependency, but he does it through his sister, Doris. They are both paternalistic racists who write off these "investments" they make and then have the gall to parade around like they are humanitarians.

It is further asserted that,

> "She doesn't hold back," Campbell said. "She's a grandmother; she says what she wants.""When you're 88, you have no filter," her grandson added with a laugh. High-profile corporate executives and the super-rich often receive financial pleas from strangers, although they are more likely to donate to charities than to private citizens, said Virginia Esposito, president of the National Center for Family Philanthropy in Washington, D.C. . (Pfeiffer, 2016)

Recall Buffett's earlier words: they don't make donations, they make "investments." And now also remember that paltry average donation of less than five thousand dollars. And now, the third strike from the previous excerpt: they are more likely to donate to charities than to private citizens. See? When all is said and done, how many black corporations or charities do you know? None. And that means that it's a case of white building no and supporting other whites. That is the Buffett method of operation, despite the minorities and low income who they pimp and placate while generating more funding.

For instance,

> "A Hewlett, a Packard, a Rockefeller — you're going to find that they get those [requests] quite a bit. So do local business people well-known in a community or a region," she said. . (Pfeiffer, 2016).

Hewlett Packard and Rockefeller are just like the Buffetts: *poverty pimps who use the fake "philanthropy" route to curry favor with the government and the community while also getting a nice tax write-off.* They are wealthy grafters, people who swindle individuals by providing them with money and then getting that money returned to them on the back end through tax write offs and other loopholes while telling the public that it's about "philanthropy."

In the meantime they can build a mailing list made up of the people who are doing the leeching. They can then use that mailing list for their own ends or sell those lists to marketing companies or anyone who wants to reach out to the American public. The article continues:

> "But this is not usually what these executives or wealthy people think of as their philanthropy," Esposito added, so "a lot of people probably ignore those letters or send back a very polite reply that they don't do giving to individuals." . (Pfeiffer, 2016).

Esposito should add that those replies are usually in the way of form letters that also have a pre-copies stamp of the signature of the funder on them. These rich people don't give a shit about anything other than the bottom line. Most of their headquarters and homes are located in areas of the nation that have large black populations and impoverished communities. But these rich people, like Warren Buffett, don't give a damn unless they can get a piece of the action through a social service or housing program where they can get their money back through the state.

In vintage "fluff piece" manner, the writer somehow locates one person who lucked out and got a grant/gift from Buffett:

> One person who benefited from their generosity is 76-year-old Mabel Willey of Searsmont, Maine, who asked for a new mobile home in 2010 ... "My trailer that I was living in was falling apart," Willey explained in a Globe interview, "and I was raising three

grandkids all by myself after their mother just walked out the door and left them." . (Pfeiffer, 2016)

An elderly woman who is probably on her death bed leeches for a new mobile home. Not a house – mobile home. She was raising her grandkids there. Now stay with me now because I believe that a scam is unraveling:

> After reviewing Willey's letter, Doris Buffett bought her a used trailer for $28,125, as well as $2,225 in furnishings from Walmart, but only after thoroughly vetting the request. . (Pfeiffer, 2016).

So they "bought" her a "used" trailer. Wonder where they got it? Could it be one of the trailers that Warren re-possessed when he foreclosed on that Mexican people down in Gallup, New Mexico? (Read my story and analysis elsewhere in this book). So that's why it was "used". Other than that why not get a brand new one and then have the woman sign papers to give it back once she dies? It was used because, in my view, it was repossessed. And then to claim that it cost over $28,000 is ludicrous. What was that – the fee to cover transportation costs to move the trailer to the elderly woman's location?

And why buy the furnishings from Walmart. And who selected those furnishings? It doesn't matter because I can answer the first question which puts the second one to rest. According to Marketwatch.com (2017):

> Buffett had been trimming his Wal-Mart exposure. The stake had been cut down to about 12.9 million shares at the end of September, after having been as high as 60.385 million shares during 2015. If Buffett had never started selling out of Wal-Mart, that 60 million share stake would be worth more than $4.3 billion in current times. Buffett still called Wal-Mart a great company and a great American success story.

There you go: Warren had major holdings for a long time. That's where the connection comes in. These Buffetts don't do anything for free. Continuing:

> "Oh my lord, they called several times — several times — and a very nice lady even came to the house," Willey recalled. "I had to tell them what I had for an income, which is no big deal — just Social Security — and why I had the children. Things like that." . (Pfeiffer, 2016).

This is racist and classist in their purest forms. In sociology we refer to this kind of response to Buffett interrogations as a "degradation ceremony," and it's a part of what we call "ingratiation theory." It is a theory that holds that,

> Ingratiation is a psychological technique in which an individual attempts to influence, manipulate or control another by becoming more attractive or likeable to their target. This term was coined by social psychologist Edward E. Jones. This outcome can be achieved by using several methods: Other enhancement is a method in which the ingratiator compliments the target individual. Opinion conformity occurs when the ingratiator adopts and validates the attitudes and beliefs of the target individual. (Wikipedia, 2017).

In this case the people who come to the Buffetts ingratiate themselves because they believe that this is what they should do in order to show the Buffetts that they are "humble and loveable," like Shoeshine Boy, the secret identity of the cartoon super hero, Underdog. In degrading themselves, they "validated the attitudes and beliefs" of people like the Buffetts, who view themselves as missionaries of sorts.

Continuing:

> "They were wonderful people to do this for me," she said. Another beneficiary of Buffett largesse is 47-year-old Michelle Sanchez of Santa Rosa, Calif., who has been in a wheelchair since 1987 because of a degenerative disease. She wanted a manual wheelchair to keep her arm muscles strong, but Medicaid would only pay for a motorized one. . (Pfeiffer, 2016)

Singular, isolated cases being held up as optimal acts of beneficence.

> So Sanchez wrote to the Buffetts and received $5,561 for a manual wheelchair, as well as a second gift of $462.50 for wheelchair side guards. . (Pfeiffer, 2016).

Did she get the cash or did she get a check made out to a wheelchair company? If it was cash, how do the Buffetts know that it was spent on what Sanchez said she was going to spend it on? And what makes her wheelchair needs any more important than the hundreds of other people who write to the Sunshine Foundation requesting cash money or some other form of assistance? Perhaps this is a lie, akin to the ones told by President Donald Trump on a regular basis?

The article closes out with vintage happy hobo-type platitudes by the woman who received the mobile home:

> "If you want something, you have to ask, and the worst somebody can say is no," Willey said. "A lot of people abuse the system and want to get things for nothing, but bad things do happen to good people — things that are out of your control." . (Pfeiffer, 2016)

Now the leech, who got a free mobile home, is now talking down to people who were in the same condition she was before she got her windfall. The Buffett family is in no way what it purports to be or what fluff pieces like the one written by Pfeiffer make it out to be.

Doris Buffett and The Sunshine Lady Foundation

Before getting into the guts of this section of the essay, let me share some generic philosophical statements made by Doris Buffett:

> We look at everything as an investment rather than a give-away. *We do hands-up, not handouts.* A grant without collaboration is a handout, and we never give a handout. We give a hand up. . .making a deal. . .Each recipient becomes our partner in the deal. We treat our partners with dignity and respect, and our joy comes from seeing them empowered by their own actions. . .She's making sure that the people she helps make good choices, by holding them accountable, and requiring them to make good decisions. (Drake, 2011 – emphasis added)

Truer words were never spoken when Doris admits, "We look at everything as an investment rather than a give-away. We do hands up, not handouts." Yeah, as in "put your hands up – this is a stickup!" These white people have been robbing poor communities blind for decades, and that is clearly established in this book. Then, after Jesse James holds up the bank he has the gall to turn to the bank manager and say, "stop ripping off the masses"!

Look at the cool and callous statements being uttered by these present-day robber barons. It is claimed, "Each recipient becomes a partner in the deal." What "deal"? They give out money with strings attached, meaning that the recipient has no rights. That kind of "partnership" is akin to the one between the farmer and the mule or better yet, the pimp and the prostitute!

Then, after this "deal" has been made, the Sunshine Lady Foundation representatives have the unmitigated gall to claim, "We treat our partners with dignity and respect, and our joy comes from seeing them empowered by their own actions. . ." There's that word "empower," the same one that Susie and her cronies stole from me after I initiated a series of "self-empowerment conferences" in the black community. Once I left for Dallas, they stole the concept, stripped off the word "self" and then came up with an "African-American Empowerment Network" which is a shill for the Sherwood Foundation which Susie Buffett controls.

An August 13, 2016 article in the Boston Globe titled, "Wanted: Help Handing Out Warren Buffett's Fortune" provides much of the information I came across regarding the "Sunshine Lady Foundation," which is headed by Buffett's sister, Doris. If fluff and candy-lined bullshit don't already permeate the life of this billionaire hustler, then let this article be yet one more example.

It begins, thusly:

> For anyone who has ever wondered what it would be like to give away millions of dollars to people in need, here's your chance to help Warren Buffett and his sister do just that. One consequence of being extremely wealthy is that strangers ask you for money — not just donation requests from countless charities, but pleas for financial help from individuals all over the world. (Pfeiffer, 2016).

These people make it sound like their "donations" are heart-felt and genuine, but they're basically tax write-offs. They contribute to you – if you have nonprofit status and their contribution is tax deductible. Or, like Susie Buffett (Warren's daughter in Omaha) does, only support those causes that receive state aid and in that way you get your "donation" returned to you on the back end.

If Buffett was going to just give away money, then since he's supposed to be so intelligent, he would give it to the people and entities who need help the most. He lives less than five miles from the largest ghetto in the state of Nebraska and all he's done is buy up property and build houses. And unless you consider a hi-rise condominium in the heart of the black community as a "donation," then it's fair to say that he pretty much hasn't done a damn thing other than bring people like Tiger Woods and Michael Jordan to town and at no time do they step foot in the black community.

And despite these facts, the website on his sister, Doris, offers the following fabricated piece of fluff regarding Warren's "beneficence:"

> The Buffett family has been **vocal in their belief in social justice**. In 2007, Mr. Buffett donated the bulk of his fortune to the Bill and Melinda Gates Foundation which does "wholesale" philanthropy ~ they **give money to organizations to dispense to individuals**. At

the same time, he pledged to fund the grant requests that came to his office **that he forwarded to his sister to be fulfilled ~ "retail" philanthropy ~ the grants are given to individuals.** Ms. Buffett seems to share her brother's frustration with people who are clueless about the link between adequate funding and social issues. Both aspire to timely make a difference ... (Drake, 2011 – emphasis added).

To begin with being "vocal" about social justice is all most white people in power ever do. They talk the talk, but they rarely walk the walk. As I have charged Warren Buffett lives in a community with the number one black child poverty rate in the nation, and there he sits, talking shit about giving money to another rich white man to disperse. This is vintage: white folks funding other white folks to sit in judgment of black folks

And the trend continues as you see that the Buffett Foundation that Warren is in charge of gives money to "organizations to dispense to individuals." Those organizations are all white. So again, these Caucasians decide and determine which people of color are "worthy" of their donations. The only thing is that most of the organizations they choose are reactionary and backwards and do little to serve the Omaha black community.

Finally, he has his sister Doris give out the money to individuals – what he calls "retail philanthropy." But it's the same racist chain of command: an elderly white woman whose been married four times sitting in her mansion with her white pals deciding who gets paid and who doesn't. Furthermore, the average allotment is only $4,800, so when he talks of "retail," he's not bullshitting. It's the same kind of cheap trick that Jewish merchants used to run on black people.

Moreover, when I say Warren Buffett exploits minorities, I'm talking about him and his entire family. I'm talking about his history, traditions, philosophy and vision.

Moving on:

> Each year, Buffett, the billionaire investor, receives thousands of letters from people asking whether he would pay their mortgages, medical bills, credit card debt, and more. Through a unique sibling partnership, Buffett forwards the letters to his older sister, Doris, who decides which ones to fund. Over the past decade, at least 22,000 letters have crossed their collective desks, and they have given away more than $12 million. . (Pfeiffer, 2016)

What does Pfeiffer mean a "Unique sibling partnership"? She's his sister by blood – what is unique about that? This glorification of this wealthy octogenarian takes place everywhere he goes, hence his title of "Oracle of Omaha." He's no "oracle" of anything except investing his money. He is as soulless and lacking in cultural compunction as any other white man.

The claim is that he and his sister "gave away more than $12 million." Again, no they did not. Giving away money is a careless act, the way Warren's daughter did when she got talked out of her panties by two bruthas and gave them $150,000 in cash to sponsor "parties" at the North Omaha YMCA so kids would stay out of trouble. Didn't this stupid bitch know that it is at these kinds of social soirees where kids GET into trouble? And why no receipt or invoice with the donation? You know why. Back to the other family member – Warren's sister:

> And now, in what might be Boston's most unusual volunteer opportunity, Doris Buffett — who moved to the city last fall — is looking for people in Greater Boston to help her read a backlog of those letters, as well as new batches that continually arrive. .
> (Pfeiffer, 2016)

Reading people's personal pleas for help – a bunch of strangers sitting in judgment of those who have less than they have. This is the same thing that the Buffett Foundation and the Sherwood Foundation do in and around Omaha, Nebraska. But there is one more addition to the scam: they don't "give" money unless there are plenty of strings attached. Most of the organizations they help are groups they end up either directly or indirectly controlling. And if a Buffett is on your board of directors, you better believe that the organization is going to be towing the line to whatever that individual wants.

And then there's the fake modesty – akin to the photos that Warren took with his arms around the shoulders of two black teenagers in front of a fire truck in Omaha the day before the Presidential election. He was in Omaha and Hillary vowed that if she won, she would dance in the streets with Warren. This, of course, after he donated millions to her campaign, set up speaking gigs for her and basically helped her go after her opponent, Donald Trump. The Buffett's don't "give away," "donate" or "contribute" money; they *invest* it.

Warren's fake modesty is equaled by that of his sister. Check it out:

> "My brother is putting up the money, so we're sort of limitless," Buffett, 88, said in an interview with the Globe. "He's told me that any time I run out of money, all I have to do is call him.". (Pfeiffer, 2016)

This woman is as old as dust – as old as Warren. They were around when racial segregation in both Omaha and Boston were the law of the land. They lived in exclusive white communities and they weren't big on civil rights issues. So when these black people get "hired" to do their bidding the way they do in Omaha, Nebraska, those are not beneficiaries of grants: those are lackeys! They are on the Buffett dole to assist in the gradual incursion into the black community!

I don't know how it is in Boston. But when I see a name like Sunshine Lady Foundation, I link it to the same grandiosity that I see when the name "Sherwood Foundation" is used in Omaha. The Sherwood Foundation is Susie's little billion dollar playpen and if you recall, Sherwood Forest was where Robin Hood and his Merry Men hung out and "stole from the rich to give to the poor." In her case, she's pimping the poor so that she can become even richer! I don't know if Warren's sister has the same approach or philosophy, but I wouldn't be the least bit surprised.

According to the article,

> Warren Buffett, the chief executive of Berkshire Hathaway Inc., has an estimated net worth of $66 billion, ranking fourth on Forbes magazine's list of the richest people in the world. . (Pfeiffer, 2016)

The process should be very simple: give the money to those who need it the most. Not those pimp charities like United Way, but to truly needy institutions. Not bullshit groups like the National Urban League or Operation PUSH. Every major city has one organization that is putting in work for the community that is barely hanging on. Buffett has people on his staff who could easily locate these entities and individuals. Instead he and his family take the grandiose route, boast about "giving away" money, pointing to all of the leech letters they've gotten, and then sit around playing god and determining who will receive funding.

If you ever wanted to know what a life of leisure was about, check out what Doris Buffett considers to be a "job":

> In recent years, Doris Buffett has had about a dozen volunteers helping her review letters in Fredericksburg, Va., where she previously lived, and Rockport, Maine, where she has a summer home. But that group has dwindled, so she wants to replenish its ranks with people from the Boston area. That proximity is important because Buffett wants volunteers who can meet with her regularly — she lives in the Back Bay — to discuss which funding requests are reasonable. . (Pfeiffer, 2016)

To begin with, a dozen "volunteers." When your last name is Buffett and your job is to give away money, the people who you "choose" to be volunteers are also wealthy – that's how they can afford to spend their time "volunteering." They are probably old white women who sit around a long table, sipping on tea and summoning the butler from time to time, cracking stale jokes and sitting in judgment of people who are starving to death or those who claim that they will "help the needy" if Doris is kind enough to give them some of Warren's dough.

The fact that she has a "summer home" shows that Doris, like her brother, is out of touch with reality and looks down her nose at the average person. These rich white people have no conscience, but only give away money in order to receive some kind of tax break or write-off. But the media, and the people who promote these "philanthropists" don't mention these realities because it runs counter to the myth of "giving" that permeates the atmosphere of one of the greediest, most conniving and money-hungry nations that ever existed.

The God complex, plain and simple. How else to explain the statement that Doris Buffett "lives in the Back Bay – to discuss which funding requests are reasonable." The fact that the requests are reasonable or not is not the point. All of them are probably reasonable. The deciding factor is if the requests are marketable and profitable to the Foundation or not! If the requests can generate the kind of publicity that in turn, will feed into the mythical legend of Warren Buffett. He needs some positive publicity because of the kinds of dirty deeds he's made and devilishly selfish projects he's funding, some of which will be pointed out in this book. In short, "what is reasonable" is in the eyes of the beholder (read: funding source).

Moving on:

> Her goal is to provide what she calls "life-changing" grants to people who, for reasons beyond their control, have fallen on hard financial times. A check from Doris Buffett is not akin to hitting the lottery; her gifts average about $4,800, although her largest to an individual was nearly $100,000. The intent is to stabilize people struggling with money woes. . (Pfeiffer, 2016).

This is a contradiction. The previous claim is that Doris' goal "is to provide what she calls life changing grants." If that is the case, then to deny someone because she and her rich volunteers think it may not be "reasonable" is a biased and bullshit philosophy. How can she change lives when she is sitting in judgment of the people who have firsthand knowledge of the people whose lives are in need of changing? She is not in the community, on the street or in the field. She's a rich white woman who is surrounded by servants and as such, should be sending people out into the field to check out the areas that the grant requests are going to serve. Anything short of that is pure bombast.

And she's doling out chump change: the average gift is a funky $4,800? Her niece gave two black men $150,000 that was not even collateralized or signed for! She gave out huge chunks to Goodwill of Omaha only to find out that she was over paying the management. One bad decision after another when it comes to Omaha. But she's in Boston and I bet that most of those grants have the Roxbury District (read: black community) as their "target" area. So for her to give out such paltry amounts is to only make the problems of poverty worse and the grant recipients *increasingly dependent!*

Her philosophy is as warped as that of her verbally stumbling brother. Check it out:

> "Bad things happen to good people, and sometimes, even if you try everything and keep plugging away, it doesn't work and you just have no options," said Noni Campbell, one of Doris Buffett's original volunteers. "When there's rent or cancer bills that have to be paid, a thousand dollars when you're in a very, very bad position in your life is like a million dollars." . (Pfeiffer, 2016)

Look at these patronizing bitches: providing the kind of pre-grant justification the way Donald Trump did when he thought he was going to lose the Presidency. What did he whine about? The system was rigged. But after he won the electoral college vote (with Hillary cleaning his clock as far as the popular vote), he hasn't uttered a bitch-like word since. That is what this volunteer is doing: basically throwing up her wrinkled hands and saying, "Oh well, we tried our best, but some people just can't be helped." This is the missionary mentality in full effect.

Losers all. It's a good thing that they have money. So let's took a look at some of the key issues that make Doris Buffett not only a hypocrite, but also someone who should be consistently monitored.

Warren Buffett: A Biographical Critique

There is nothing in Warren Buffett's life in Omaha that shows that he gave a shit about the black community, the status of low-income people, or the segregation that permeated the city of his birth. In fact, many of his organizational affiliations and choices are borderline racist: from fraternity affiliations to choices of where he attended college. On the other hand, maybe he didn't have the time because he was too busy living in fear of his own mother. In fact, he was a sissy – a coward, even as a young boy:

> Although Mrs. Buffett made her son Warren cry too, she was less hard on him: As a young boy, he said he often felt the urge to protect his older sister. "But I never did, because I was afraid of becoming the target myself." Once he ran away from home to [Washington, D.C. to] escape her rants. . . "Warren was a boy, and boys, in mother's viewpoint, were more valuable than women." (Drake, 2011).

This spoiled punk even shows some of these sheepish and timid attributes to this very day. He runs away from home to escape his own mother's "rants." His mother was no prize either, contending that boys were more valuable than women. This is that Donald Trump/American misogyny bullshit full bore. He talks that liberal shit, but there is nothing courageous about Warren Buffett. And there are some facts in this book that will make this point quite clear.

Warren was a victim of child abuse for the most part:

> Roberta (Bertie) Buffett Elliott, the youngest child, escaped her mother's abuse and was sent to Northwestern University where earned a Phi Beta Kappa key. In public, Mrs. Buffett was "vivacious" and presented a "totally sunny disposition." Her great-grandson, Alexander Buffett Rozek, adored her. Their father, stockbroker and Rep. Howard Homan Buffett (R-NE), gave his children "enormous approval." Although he warned his children when his wife was on a rampage, he did nothing to protect them. While he served four terms in Congress, the family lived in Fredericksburg, VA. Omaha was their home base.(Drake, 2011).

The whole family, despite having money, was screwed up from top to bottom. And this is a common theme running through a lot of these suburbanite Omaha white folks. They have the big houses and the high status zip codes, but when you visit their homes you often find many problems. Very little furniture that doesn't match, poorly kept and maintained, bare refrigerators and so on – just to keep up an image. The kids are suffering on the inside but on the outside, as far as the schools and society are concerned, they've got it going on.

At any rate, here's some additional background information for your perusal:

> Buffett was born in 1930 in Omaha, Nebraska, of distant French Huguenot descent.[17] He was the second of three children and the only son of Leila (née Stahl) and Congressman Howard Buffett Buffett began his education at Rose Hill Elementary School. In

> 1942, his father was elected to the first of four terms in the United States Congress, and after moving with his family to Washington, D.C., Warren finished elementary school, attended Alice Deal Junior High School and graduated from Woodrow Wilson High School in 1947, where his senior yearbook picture reads: "likes math; a future stockbroker."

Nothing about civil rights involvement at all. And yet these black people in Omaha kiss his ass every time they get a chance. That is, when he allows them to get close enough. When he was speaking at North High School in August of 2016 on behalf of Hillary Clinton (who was in Omaha to leech for his money), he looked like he had just gotten ass-fucked by the 49er football team. He had no respect for his venue and he didn't say a damn thing about any issues that even remotely pertained to black people, the same ones that had stood silent all those years while he made his billions.

This muthafucka was too busy trying to make money to be concerned about people who didn't have any money at all. This is his legacy. So this shit about him talking about giving all his money away should be qualified: he's giving it away to another rich peckerwood, Bill Gates, and not to any organizations that could improve the life chances of the 50,000 black people that live less than ten miles from this ofay octogenarian's home.

Continuing:

> After finishing high school and finding success with his side entrepreneurial and investment ventures, Buffett wanted to skip college to go directly into business but was overruled by his father.

One racist hand washes the other. His father's objections were probably backed up with threats of pulling back funding support for his ventures. So rather than go into the real world broke, Warren did the intelligent thing, kept his big mouth shut, and listened to "daddy dearest" bark out orders. Still, no mention of anything even remotely associated with human or civil rights.

Moving on:

> Buffett displayed an interest in business and investing at a young age. Much of Buffett's early childhood years were enlivened with entrepreneurial ventures. One of his first business ventures, Buffett sold chewing gum, Coca-Cola bottles, or weekly magazines door to door. He worked in his grandfather's grocery store. While still in high school, he made money delivering newspapers, selling golf balls and stamps, and detailing cars, among other means. On his

> first income tax return in 1944, Buffett took a $35 deduction for
> the use of his bicycle and watch on his paper route.

Neither his biographers, his publicists or anyone who knows him mentions the terms "civil rights" or "black people" when they discuss him. That is simply because Buffett is not interested in either. He simply wants to make money, and although he is quick to insult and put down Donald Trump, these mega-rich white boys know full well that there are no people of color in their worldview other than the people they bilk, exploit and pimp. If there is a dime to be made and it involves people of color, Buffett doesn't go directly into the community where they live; he hired flunkies and desperate fake "leaders" to do his bidding. This point will be brought out in this book.

The previous biographical blurb sounds so innocent. And it is aimed at showing him as a young man by emphasizing everything that he deemed important. Do you see any mention of a person of color anywhere on it? And as I stated earlier, this old peckerwood has been living less than five miles from the state of Nebraska's largest (and only) black community most of his life, and he hasn't done a damn thing other than to most recently buy a big chunk of land on which he can construct condos and then sell/rent to people who want to "invade" North Omaha so they can be close to the jobs downtown, the airport and the Missouri River.

He's a businessman, and this means he is an exploiter of opportunity. And since white people mimic the white model of "business," the same applies to them. The black businessman pimps his own people, the Latino businessman pimps his people (although the Latino has the advantage of restaurants and white folks are obsessed with what they call "Mexican Food"), and the white man pimps them all. In the name of "business" the white man continually does what it takes to make his money. In the meantime a certain type of white man – the Jew – bilks and hoodwinks them all. I have yet to determine what kind of stranglehold those Jews and Israel have on this American white man to be able to infiltrate his ranks, dominate his banks, rip him off for billions and then get away with a slap on the wrist or maybe an arrest – that is AFTER he's sent millions back to Israel.

At any rate,

> In 1945, as a high school sophomore, Buffett and a friend spent
> $25 to purchase a used pinball machine, which they placed in the
> local barber shop. Within months, they owned several machines in
> three different barber shops across Omaha. The business was sold
> later in the year for $1,200 to a war veteran.

What is meant by "across Omaha" is more likely than not in areas that do not include the black community. At that time segregation was sky high and Buffett was a part of it and could have cared less. It is clear that those machines were for the kids whose parents could afford to give them money and that didn't include black parents. Buffett was aware of that because he was attending a segregated high school. Did he care? Of course not, and cannot be blamed for being as racist as his white school pals. But that is the point: throughout his life he has been the rule rather than the exception. No matter what he does, no matter how philanthropic it may look, this white man is going to do what's best for his race first and foremost. More on that later.

Continuing:

> Buffett's interest in the stock market and investing dated to schoolboy days he spent in the customers' lounge of a regional stock brokerage near his father's own brokerage office. On a trip to New York City at age ten, he made a point to visit the New York Stock Exchange. At 11, he bought three shares of Cities Service Preferred for himself, and three for his sister Doris Buffett (founder of The Sunshine Lady Foundation.

There is nothing in Buffett's background that shows that he ever gave a damn about people of color, poverty or civil rights. So when you read about him walking around Omaha (the white sections) with people like Michael Jordan, Tiger Woods and LeBron James, these are nothing but photo ops. And with the possible exception of LeBron, these are basically millionaire "coons" who feel proud to be in Buffett's company and none of them, including LeBron, probably even asked, "hey, where's the black community in Omaha?"

And if they did ask, what would Buffett more than likely say? He would have to point and say "it's over there, not many blacks – lots of poverty." And if one of these negroes asked what he was doing to address it, he would more than likely mention the work of his daughter Susie, masquerading her incursions and takeovers of child care by talking about Edu-Care, her co-optation of black teens with her work at Girls, Inc. and North Star, which bills itself as "the only single sex boys only after school program in Omaha." He would point to Goodwill and maybe a few charities and that would be that. Warren Buffett is the personification of Omaha and, along with other fuddy-duddies like the World Herald's Harold Anderson, Mutual of Omaha's V.J. Skutt, and others, spent his life making sure that Omaha's segregation remained "America's best kept secret." Their words, not mine.

More on Buffett's childhood continues:

> At the age of 15, Warren made more than $175 monthly delivering *Washington Post* newspapers. In high school, he invested in a business owned by his father and bought a 40-acre farm worked by a tenant farmer. He bought the land when he was 14 years old with $1,200 of his savings. By the time he finished college, Buffett had accumulated more than $90,000 in savings measured in 2009 dollars.

At no point do they mention any "help" he may have gotten from "Pops" Buffett. They make it sound like he was a self-made man. This is bullshit. This white man was born with a silver spoon in his mouth, was surrounded by fellow whites all his life, and had the benefit of white privilege. I write these words to counter that international title that was given to Warren Buffett as "the oracle of Omaha." In my book, a more accurate label would be "river city racist."

Moreover,

> In 1947, Buffett entered the Wharton School of the University of Pennsylvania. He would have preferred to focus on his business ventures; however, he enrolled due to pressure from his father ... Warren studied there for two years and joined the Alpha Sigma Phi fraternity ... He then transferred to the University of Nebraska–Lincoln where at 19, he graduated with a Bachelor of Science in Business Administration. After being rejected by Harvard Business School, Buffett enrolled at Columbia Business School upon learning that Benjamin Graham taught there. He earned a Master of Science in Economics from Columbia in 1951. Buffett also attended the New York Institute of Finance.

When a document says that you "attended" a college or university, that means you didn't finish. I "attended" the University of Iowa, the University of Illinois-Circle Campus, Diablo Valley College, Los Medanos College, Kirkwood College and several others, and got credits from them. Do I mention them? Very rarely. If you don't finish, then what is there to brag or boast about?

Furthermore, you see what Buffett's first choice was: the same racist school that President Donald Trump attended, the Wharton School of the University of Pennsylvania. And Buffett did it because his father FORCED him to. A frat boy while there for only two years, he was just another homoerotic rabble rouser. Alpha Sigma Phi, the 10th oldest fraternity in the United States, is racist and exclusive as are most white fraternities.

And check this out: Wikipedia reminds us that, "The fraternity practices many traditions. Its Latin motto is *Causa Latet Vis Est Notissima* ("The cause is hidden, the results well-known"). I'll bet the cause is "hidden" because they don't want the world to see them as the white supremacist adjunct that they are. Along with Ted Cassidy (who played "Lurch" on "The Adams Family,"), Dr. C. Everett Koop, former surgeon general and Press Maravich (father of NBA great "Pistol Pete" Maravich), Warren Buffett, to this very day, is listed as one of the school's impressive alumni.

These white boy frats are exclusively white and are racist to the core. A recent example can be found on the campus of the University of Oklahoma – the same frat, just a different campus. Under the headline, "Oklahoma In Trouble After Fraternity Posts Snapchat In White Robe." Check out this February 11, 2016 blurb from a website, Co-Ed, that covers college news all over the nation:

> The University of Oklahoma's Alpha Sigma Phi fraternity is in trouble today after a Snapchat photo depicting a brother in white robes was sent to members of African American student organization, who then demanded answers from their school. The answer they got was probably one that they were expecting, but not ready to believe: there was no racial motivation behind the photo or robe at all. (Coed, 2016).

These chapters are all in it together. They are like a white cult: selective, frivolous and geared toward freakishness and frolic. They help each other study (read: cheat) for tests and they have absolutely no respect for women. Those white robes may not have represented anything anti-black but if you are pro-white then the hatred of all else is part of the plan. Buffett belonged then, and it was by choice. He was recruited and went through "hazing" which probably included some homoerotic bullshit because that is what those white boys do. And can there be any doubt that he contributes his money (probably under the table) to the fraternity to this very day?

As for the Oklahoma version of Alpha Sigma Phi,

> According to both OU officials and Alpha Sigma Phi officials, the fraternity held an initiation ceremony over the weekend which is where the Snapchat was taken. For our readers who never joined a fraternity, it's commonplace for fraternities to use robes such as this (albeit in different colors) as part of the ceremony (which is extremely boring) that initiates pledges into brothers.(Coed, 2016).

I don't care what those writers say about how commonplace these fraternity robes are. It is also "commonplace" for these white assholes to get involved in the racial harassment of black women and it is also commonplace for their members to rape white girls inside of those fraternity houses. Buffett knows this, but he keeps it quiet, just as he masks some of his chickenshit ways and racist activities that I have uncovered in this book.

With that having been shared, we can now move on.

When you have that much money you are always going to get kudos. I learned the hard way, that the media is so fascinated with wealth that rarely will they "dig deep" and try to find out about the local activities of these men and women who grow to be "celebrities." I found that out about people like Michael Jordan, Johnny Rodgers, Kathy Hughes, and a host of other people who had fame, but could have cared less about black people.

Warren Buffett, in my view, falls into this category.

> Warren Edward Buffett born August 30, 1930) is an American business magnate, investor and philanthropist. He is considered by some to be one of the most successful investors in the world. Buffett is the chairman, CEO and largest shareholder of Berkshire Hathaway, and is consistently ranked among the world's wealthiest people. He was ranked as the world's wealthiest person in 2008 and as the third wealthiest in 2015. In 2012 *Time* named Buffett one of the world's most influential people. (Wikipedia, 2016).

There may be a reason why Buffett totally ignored the segregated state of Omaha, the city of his birth. Today in 2016 he talks about donating some of his money to the world, but he didn't think about making any contributions to the black community of Omaha, which was less than five miles from his home. He never contributed to bail out black organizations, museums or any endeavor that might have kept North Omaha from becoming number one in the nation in black child poverty, which is its current ranking.

It is because of people like Warren Buffett (and Johnny Rodgers, Bob Boozer, Bob Gibson, Kathy Hughes) and other black Omahans who rose to fame that I always doubt a black person's real "celebrity." My first question is, what has this person contributed to his community? What has he done to help local black folk? So when I see people like Michael Jordan and LeBron James coming to Omaha with Buffett, I realize what is taking place: it's window dressing of some kind. None of the people he brings to Omaha are ever brought to the ghetto to see its condition and learn about how he is buying up property there so he can make money. Elsewhere in this book I document cases where he doesn't care who he exploits, as long as he makes money.

Omaha was his training ground. As Wikipedia points out,

> Buffett is often referred to as the "Wizard of Omaha" or "Oracle of Omaha," or the "Sage of Omaha," and is noted for his adherence to value investing and for his personal frugality despite his immense wealth. Buffett is a notable philanthropist, having pledged to give away 99 percent of his fortune to philanthropic causes, primarily via the Gates Foundation. (Wikipedia, 2016).

He knows that he is about to die. During a speech he gave when Hillary Clinton came to town (to leech for some of his political campaign money), he had the nerve to take the podium. He looked and sounded like shit, as if he was on his last legs. So any pledge to give away his money is bullshit: he might "invest" his money, but if he was going to give it away, why not give it the local people of color who are living in poverty? Why is his daughter buying up property all over the ghetto and then providing early education to black kids who are Title XX eligible so she can make her money back from the state? No matter how much money you have, a racist is a racist is a racist.

And with all that money, you just can't escape death when it comes knocking at your door. Recall that about four years ago, Buffett – despite all of his money and access to top flight medical care – was diagnosed with cancer. As one source reminds us,

> On April 11, 2012, he was diagnosed with prostate cancer, for which he successfully completed treatment in September 2012. Buffett is also active in contributing to political causes, having endorsed Democratic candidate Hillary Clinton for president during the 2016 campaign season. (Wikipedia, 2016).

To begin with, this was about the same time that his greedy ass daughter was given more power to invade the black community and continue buying up land and housing. Though stricken and ill, her father is now building a giant condominium project called "75 North" and again, this is not about charitable giving; it is about making money and helping the return of white folks back to the black area of town that they abandoned when they found out that black people were coming in. It's known as "white flight."

He is the founder and president of Berkshire Hathaway, and they are buying up houses and land all over the low-income area of Omaha and, from what I can tell, in other cities as well. In addition to being poverty pimps and paternalistic racists as I have alleged, they are also land grabbers. As Wikipedia documents it, "Buffett worked from 1951 to 1954 at Buffett-Falk & Co. as an investment salesman; from 1954 to 1956 at Graham-Newman Corp. as a securities analyst; from 1956 to 1969 at Buffett Partnership, Ltd. as a general partner and from 1970, as Chairman and CEO of Berkshire Hathaway Inc." Through the years while he was working with other rich white dudes, he was saving his money. By 1956, Benjamin Graham, one of those bosses, retired and closed his partnership. At this time "Buffett's personal savings were over $174,000 ($1.47 million 2012 USD) and he started Buffett Partnership Ltd.." (Wikipedia, 2017).In 1962, Buffett became a millionaire because of his partnerships, which in January 1962 had an excess of $7,178,500, of which over $1,025,000 belonged to Buffett. (Wikipedia, 2017).

According to Wikipedia,

> Buffett became a paper billionaire when Berkshire Hathaway began selling class A shares on May 29, 1990, with the market closing at US$7,175 a share … In 1998 he acquired General Re (Gen Re) as a subsidiary in a deal that presented difficulties—according to the *Rational Walk* investment website, "underwriting standards proved to be inadequate," while a "problematic derivatives book" was resolved after numerous years and a significant loss … Gen Re later provided reinsurance after Buffett became involved with Maurice R. Greenberg at AIG in 2002 (Wikipedia, 2017).

Hooking up with Jewish millionaires – the same strategy that Donald Trump describes in the first forty or so pages of his book, The Art of the Deal. Buffett may have been raised in Omaha, but he was not OF Omaha. He didn't care about any social issues at all and as you can see, even in the early days as Omaha segregation persisted, he could have cared less.

Continuing:

> Buffett married Susan Buffett (née Thompson) in 1952. They had three children, Susie, Howard and Peter. The couple began living separately in 1977, although they remained married until Susan Buffett's death in July 2004. Their daughter, Susie, lives in Omaha, is a national board member of Girls, Inc., and does charitable work through the Susan A. Buffett Foundation … (Wikipedia, 2017).

This is what happens when you're a billionaire and everyone around you, including Wikipedia, is competing to kiss your ass. What you just read in the preceding excerpt is biographically true and morally flawed.

For instance, who gives a damn if Susie is on the board of directors of Girls, Inc., when she is also doing dirt in and around the black community of Omaha by buying up property, lots and old houses and then re-selling them and otherwise making them available to young white people who want to move into the inner city even as black people are being relocated? Who cares about her "charitable work" when she is doling out $150 in cash to two young bruthas with no contract, no receipt and then when caught says her strategy was to give them the money so that they could throw weekend parties at the local high school "to keep black kids out of trouble"?

Oh, and an update. In April of 2017 the case of all that money being given to those two black men somehow ended up in court. The streets say that it was because Warren demanded that Susie take legal action. It took place in 2015 and finally appeared in an article under the headline, "Cousins didn't mean to deceive Sherwood Foundation, judge rules, dismissing theft charges." These Omaha white women and their black fantasies, always covered up by the media and the powerful. Check out the following newspaper account:

> And it was *the nebulous nature of the transaction among two Omaha cousins*, a nonprofit led by Susie Buffett and a middleman that led the criminal fraud case against the men to crumble, a Douglas District Court judge suggested last week when he dismissed the theft charges that had been filed against them. (Clarridge, 2015 – emphasis added).

No, it was the "nebulous nature of the transaction between Susie Buffett and those two niggas" that Omaha was trying to cover up! No signed contracts, no invoices, no legacies of wills: just a rich white woman "for some reason" giving up cash to two bruthas. Again, the newspaper account:

> In using the roughly $150,000 that they received from the Sherwood Foundation to, as one of them termed it, "better their lives," the cousins, Quincey L. Louis and Latron D. Louis, may have not spent the money as the group intended, to host parties for youths in north and South Omaha. And they may well find themselves in civil court to argue the terms of their agreements with the foundation.

What terms of their agreement with the foundation? If there were stated terms and an agreement, then what was all the rancor and rigmarole about? Now, more on the case:

> The case began when the cousins presented the Sherwood Foundation with a six-month business plan. They would organize and promote monthly parties, safe spaces for teenagers to gather at YMCAs, and Sherwood would help fund the events. The foundation had given the cousins' business roughly $60,000 to

> fund similar events in 2014. Latron Louis, a former gang member, met Buffett around 2007. (Clarridge, 2015).

Yeah – he "met" her alright. Louis runs ads in my nationally recognized newsletter every month, and runs a t-shirt shop. He's the person that Susie trusted with her money. As for that business plan: more than likely it was a piece of shit, hastily thrown together and just handed over so that there would be something, anything, on the record books before Susie handed over more than $150,00 – the SECOND time she gave a young black man money with no real collateral. Black men and women know what to call this because we've seen it before. The major media shirks it because her last name is Buffett, just like the media over looks the racist abuse of those Mexicans down in Gallup, Mexico that Warren is guilty of.

The story about the "grant money" continues:

> The Sherwood board reviewed the half-year budget request and doubled it. The foundation pledged $150,620 to the Louis cousins, but there was no formal contract and few strings were attached. The foundation grew concerned when the cousins cashed checks it provided through a third party. (Clarridge, 2015).

The key is that there was no "formal contract." Why not? What were the terms? Did she know these guys well enough to make such a commitment? Of course she did. How well she knew them remains to be seen, but black people know what time it is: Omaha is filled with white women paying black men for various "favors." It's g going on at Creighton, at UNO and in the community where black kids are driving around in the sport cars of white suburban women. And we know what's at the basis of it.

It is clear that Susie violated her father's basic premise: we don't "give" money, we "invest" it. And even she does the same when it comes to buying up land and building grant-generating nonprofits in the black community. Why was there a deviation from the rules in this particular case? Here are some more facts:

> In an interview with police, Latron Louis indicated he and his cousin thought of the money as personal income earned in exchange for producing the events. They charged admission for the parties, and they planned to use those door proceeds to pay for security, food and other expenses. Confronted by Buffett and the foundation about how the funds were handled, Latron Louis presented them with a copy of a bank statement that showed $100,000 in a Wells Fargo account belonging to Quincey Louis, a police detective testified. But an investigation by the bank revealed the account really contained only $100, the detective testified.

In his order, Bataillion wrote there was no evidence of criminal intent. (Clarridge, 2015).

So Louis "conned" her. So what? I met that young brutha before and in fact, ran free ads for him in my two-time national finalist newsletter, the TONA News. He couldn't receive a check that wasn't written out for him and then handed to him. Those are the facts that white people continue to overlook in their "grievances." What the white man responds to when it comes to blonde hair, long legs and a mini-skirt is akin to what white women respond to when they see a black man and can't help staring at his bulge.

Continuing:

> But the Louises did not commit felony theft by deception, the crime with which each was charged in April, Judge Peter Bataillon ruled. "Misusing the money and deceiving to obtain the money are two separate and distinct actions," Bataillon wrote in response to a challenge of the evidence by the Louises' attorneys."I suffered a lot going through this situation," Quincey Louis said Wednesday. "There was no wrongdoing." (Clarridge, 2015).

There was some wrongdoing, but not the kind that was expected by Warren Buffett, who forced Susie to pursue charges. It was a white bitch giving a bunch of cash money to some niggas, the way they do in most major cities around the country. It's called the pimp-prostitute relationship and it is these kind of women who get "turned out" and make fortunes for worthless black men who waste the money on jewelry, clothing and various forms of conspicuous consumption. From New York,, Philly, Detroit, L.A. and even Omaha – "don't hate the playa – hate the game."

Such idiocy is covered up by the local media and the Buffetts get major space to point the finger at other people. Such as was the case when Susie was making donations to Goodwill only to find out that the CEO was raking in hundreds of thousands of dollars in salary.

Continuing:

> In 2006, on his 76th birthday, Buffett married his longtime companion, Astrid Menks, who was then 60 years old—she had lived with him since his wife's departure to San Francisco in 1977 … Susan had arranged for the two to meet before she left Omaha to pursue her singing career. All three were close and Christmas cards to friends were signed "Warren, Susie and Astrid".[86] Susan briefly discussed this relationship in an interview on the *Charlie*

Rose Show shortly before her death, in a rare glimpse into Buffett's personal life ... (Wikipedia, 2017).

You can believe one thing: there was a prenuptial agreement! That old fart got married because he needed some companionship and his health is probably in question. This "longtime companion" is what you call her when she's screwing someone with Buffett's money. If she was the streets she'd be called what she is: a ho! Is there any doubt he was messing around with her even WHILE he was married? You see, when you have money, the newspapers and the websites all want to kiss your ass and deal with white life as if it is nothing more than a series of highlights. That's why I'm writing this book: to show you that when all is said and done, the self-proclaimed "oracle of Omaha" is really nothing more than a "river city racist."

Buffett is low-down, for the most part. Like many rich people, the philosophy he lives by is "my way, or the highway." Observe the following:

> Buffett disowned his son Peter's adopted daughter, Nicole, in 2006 after she participated in the Jamie Johnson documentary *The One Percent.* Although his first wife referred to Nicole as one of her "adored grandchildren" ... Buffett wrote her a letter stating, "I have not emotionally or legally adopted you as a grandchild, nor have the rest of my family adopted you as a niece or a cousin" ...(Wikipedia, 2017).

See how the major media covers up this asshole's "real side"? He's being dubbed "the oracle of Omaha," but it seems to me that "the ogre of Omaha" would be more suiting. In the same way that Donald Trump's horrific past and on-going scamming of people was kept under wraps for the most part, it's even worse in the case of Buffett. He's dubbed the world's richest man but as a human being it is clear that he is cold, calculating and, in the words of the ghetto, "quite chickenshit." Look how he treats his own people: how do you "disown" someone who was adopted by your own son? While black men get castigated for being "absentee fathers" and "deadbeat dads," this rich sonofabitch is pulling this kind of thing and getting away with it because the media is afraid of him and they need his advertising revenue.

Moving right along:

> Buffett is an avid bridge player, which he plays with fellow fan Gates - he allegedly spends 12 hours a week playing the game.[98]
> In 2006, he sponsored a bridge match for the Buffett Cup. Modeled on the Ryder Cup in golf—held immediately before it in the same

> city—the teams are chosen by invitation, with a female team and five male teams provided by each country …

The "Gates" being referred to is billionaire Bill Gates. That is what these imperialists do: play cards and discuss new ways to maintain control over the niggas. That's what they do. In this document I show how Buffett exploits Mexican Indians through his trailer parks and he and his daughter are doing the same thing here in Omaha with their takeovers of the land and housing in the black community. Gates gives lectures all over the continent of Africa making promises about improving the health of the continent while also giving out computers to America's inner cities. But these social service-type actions do not make either of these men any less racist. After all, Heinrich Himmler (of the Nazi Party of Germany) loved animals and I'm sure that members of the KKK attend church on Sunday.

This old white man has had his misgiving covered up by the Nebraska and national media all of his life. All you read about him are bullshit "by the way" trivia type fluff pieces designed to make him look like "an average Joe," like in the reference to his playing bridge that we read about earlier. Moreover,

> He is a dedicated, lifelong follower of Nebraska football, and attends as many games as his schedule permits. He supported the hire of Bo Pelini, following the 2007 season, stating, "It was getting kind of desperate around here" … He watched the 2009 game against Oklahoma from the Nebraska sideline, after being named an honorary assistant coach … (Wikipedia, 2017).

He may attend the games but felt he was too good to attend UN-L as a student. He attends the games because it is the only game in the entire state – literally. These cornhusking hicks don't have a pro team, and therefore they flock from hundreds of miles around to make the drive up I-80 to see the Nebraska Cornhuskers play on Saturday. In fact, these hillbillies are known as one of the top fan bases in the country, driving to faraway places like Miami, Penn State and Texas to follow a COLLEGE football team.

"Honorary assistant coach"? That's like making Mr. Smithers the starting point guard for the Golden State Warriors! What does this old white man know about football strategy? He's spent his entire sheltered life exploiting other people. He is no "mentor" or "coach" or "manager" of any kind. This is what is covered up and this is what this short book is working to expose. He is no "Oracle of Omaha"; he's a "River City racist"!

But even a billionaire can't buy good health. As Wikipedia (2017) documents it,

> On April 11, 2012, Buffett was diagnosed with stage I prostate cancer during a routine test … He announced he would begin two months of daily radiation treatment from mid-July; however, in a letter to shareholders, Buffett said he felt "great - as if I were in my normal excellent health - and my energy level is 100 percent". On September 15, 2012, Buffett announced that he had completed the full 44-day radiation treatment cycle, saying "it's a great day for me" and "I am so glad to say that's over" …(Wikipedia, 2017).

All that money and access to resources and this old fuddy duddy didn't even have the wherewithal to get regular checkups for prostate cancer? All those connections throughout the medical community and he didn't know that the older you get the more likely you are to get prostate cancer? An educated fool except when it comes to making money. He is willing to even ignore his own health care needs in his quest for the almighty dollar. That is what the previous passage of information clearly shows. And he's so happy because he dodged a bullet and in the meantime, he's making life a living hell for people of color in various parts of the country.

Furthermore,

> In 2008 he was ranked by *Forbes* as the richest person in the world with an estimated net worth of approximately US$62 billion … In 2009, after donating billions of dollars to charity, Buffett was ranked as the second richest man in the United States with a net worth of US$37 billion … with only Bill Gates ranked higher than Buffett. His net worth had risen to $58.5 billion as of September 2013 … (Wikipedia, 2017).

Both Gates and Buffett have something in common: they are both experts at bullshitting the American and international media and as a result, the public. All that money and no one has the guts to report on how Buffett has bilked low income minorities in New Mexico or is landgrabbing and taking over a black community in Omaha, Nebraska through his equally selfish daughter, Susie. American capitalism at its finest.

Not only is he a capitalist, but he's also a cold-blooded asshole. Check out the following statement he made about cigarettes:

> During the RJR Nabisco, Inc. hostile takeover fight in 1987, Buffett was quoted as telling John Gutfreund … I'll tell you why I

like the cigarette business. It costs a penny to make. Sell it for a
dollar. It's addictive. And there's fantastic brand loyalty.— *Buffett,
quoted in Barbarians at the Gate: The Fall of RJR Nabisco*
(Wikipedia, 2017).

The profit margin at any cost. This is the thinking of a kleptocrat. Does he care about the long-term impact or effects? He knew about cigarettes causing cancer even has he was uttering these words. But what was his primary concern: the bottom line. He knows about addiction and how those who can control the people who are addicted can make money. That's what dope dealers do. He may call it a "fantastic brand loyalty" but behind every Marlboro, Camel, Kool, Benson & Hedges, and all of the rest, lies someone who is killing him/herself with every puff. "He who has the ability to satisfy human needs controls the humans that have those needs."

This is akin to the way that President Donald Trump reacted when a prominent Saudi journalist was killed in the Saudi embassy and then dismembered. Congress was supposedly "outraged" but what was the response of the head "kleptocrat"? Trump said that he wasn't going to take any stpes to halt arms sales and military support to Saudi Arabia: ""What good does that do us?" Mr. Trump asked, speaking to reporters midday in the Oval Office." Trump further explained,

> "I would not be in favor of stopping a country from spending $110 billion — which is an all-time record — and letting Russia have that money and letting China have that money," Mr. Trump said, referring to an arms deal with the Saudis, brokered last year, that the president has said will lead to new American jobs. (Wong, Schmitt & Sullivan, 2018)

This is what kleptocrats do: they place money and profits over human life. Now let's reflect back to Warren Buffett's earlier statement – the previous quote about cigarettes, profits and addiction goes directly to the character (or lack thereof) of Warren Buffett, plain and simple. And the only time he second-guesses anything is if it's something that may decline in value somewhere in the future. For instance,

> Speaking at Berkshire Hathaway Inc.'s 1994 annual meeting, Buffett said investments in tobacco are: fraught with questions that relate to societal attitudes and those of the present administration. I would not like to have a significant percentage of my net worth invested in tobacco businesses. The economy of the business may be fine, but that doesn't mean it has a bright future.

— *Buffett, Berkshire Hathaway annual meeting.* (Wikipedia, 2017).

This is not even close to a moral stand. This asshole knew what cigarettes could do to the human body and he therefore had to know that the marketers were aiming at the youth market. Did that stop him? Of course not. And it only "slowed him down" because he projected some economic changes in the future. And even in that you don't see anything definitive about the link between cancer and cigarettes.

This is the REAL Warren Buffett, and now we get to the racist nature of the so-called "oracle of Omaha."

Warren Buffett: Exploitation of Minorities

The Omaha World Herald has long carried water for the powers that be. Warren Buffett is no exception which explains why the stories of the "dirt" he is pulling against people of color, not only in the city of Omaha but elsewhere, hardly makes the news. That is why it is up to progressive-thinking scholars to pull down the veil of deception that permeates the Omaha white power structure.

If there is such a thing as a "mini-kleptocracy" or a "regional kleptocracy," then Buffett has certainly been the leader of such a system for many years. You can decide what you think.

It involves the story of Clayton Homes in Gallup, New Mexico. And here is an idea of Buffett's attitude when it comes to his abuse and exploitation of that segment and his domination of the mobile-home industry:

> Buffett leads the investment conglomerate Berkshire Hathaway, which bought Clayton Homes in 2003 and spent billions building it into the mobile-home industry's biggest manufacturer and lender. Buffett told shareholders recently that he makes "no apologies whatsoever about Clayton's lending terms." (Baker, 2015).

"No apologies whatsoever." No matter what the political affiliation, can you see how these rich white boys seem to share the same "I do whatever I want" attitude? Buffett sound s like Donald Trump, does he not. The crimes that Trump has committed, from real estate fraud, employment discrimination and in my view, treason, are no different than those committed by Buffett. The difference is that

Trump's ego got him to run for President and now his crimes are open; Buffett's remain well hidden.

Until now.

Here is a man who is a billionaire and who boasts and allows the media to spread information about his so-called "philanthropy." But, as is the case of most white people who have great wealth, there is a schizophrenic nature to the way that they allocate their money. I've pointed out the Lady Sunshine Foundation and how Warren's sister Doris doles out chump change and then has the gall to brag about it; I document herein how his daughter Susie uses the same maternalistic racism to control a number of nonprofits in and around Omaha. But what about the so-called "oracle of Omaha" – or is he closer to being what I have dubbed him, "the River City racist"?

Clayton Homes in Gallup, New Mexico: Native Americans

Ironically while watching an old movie, "White Heat" (James Cagney, Edmond O'Brien) from 1949, a jail break was reported on the radio and it mentioned "Gallup, New Mexico." Surely the demographics have changed since then, but the new "criminals" are more sophisticated and in fact, led by billionaire Warren Buffett.

These mobile homes in New Mexico, controlled by Warren Buffett, are but one example of how Buffett continues to exploit people of color. Baker & Wagner (2016) note the following:

> Clayton Homes has used a pattern of deceptions to help extract billions from poor customers around the country — particularly people of color, who make up a substantial and growing portion of its business. The company is controlled by Warren Buffett, one of world's richest men. (Baker & Wagner, 2016).

Buffett doesn't just enter into business deals blindly. In fact, he's a master speculator. And he saw money to be made by exploiting minorities and he's setting up a similar system in Omaha (more on that later). The following story is so typical of how Buffett's flunkies set up the poor by feeding them air sandwiches and hope pudding about how wonderful the future will be (akin to the same lie that his daughter is feeding to "negro" Omahans even as these words are being written in 2017).

> GALLUP, N.M. — After a few years living with her sister, Rose Mary Zunie, 59, was ready to move into a place of her own. So, on

an arid Saturday morning this past summer, the sisters piled into a friend's pickup truck and headed for a mobile-home sales lot here just outside the impoverished Navajo reservation. (Baker & Wagner, 2016).

In Omaha the target is the largest black community in the entire state, and it too is "impoverished." Now, we move back to the New Mexico situation:

The women — one in a long, colorful tribal skirt, another wearing turquoise jewelry, a traditional talisman against evil — were steered to a salesman who spoke Navajo, just like the voice on the store's radio ads. He walked them through Clayton-built homes on the lot, then into the sales center, passing a banner and posters promoting one subprime lender: Vanderbilt Mortgage, a Clayton subsidiary. Inside, he handed them a Vanderbilt sales pamphlet. "Vanderbilt is the only one that finances on the reservation," he told the women. His claim, which the women caught on tape, was a lie. And it was illegal. (Baker & Wagner, 2016).

If the salesman lied, then that makes Buffett culpable as well. But the World-Herald isn't going to print anything about Omaha's icon. But I will. Check it out:

It is just one in a pattern of deceptions that Clayton has used to help extract billions from poor customers around the country — particularly people of color, who make up a substantial and growing portion of its business. **The company is controlled by Warren Buffett, one of the world's richest men, but its methods hardly match Buffett's honest, folksy image: Clayton systematically pursues unwitting minority homebuyers and baits them into costly subprime loans, many of which are doomed to fail, an investigation by The Seattle Times and BuzzFeed News has found.** (Baker & Wagner, 2016 - emphasis added)

Recall the words "honest, folksy image." That is an image built up by the white money-hungry media, the Omaha World Herald in particular. They know how crooked Buffett is and they know that there is not a single billionaire who got there through strictly honest means. The Seattle Times has far more credibility than the World Herald, the latter whose reporters rarely if ever engage in anything even remotely resembling investigative reporting.

Back to Clayton and Buffett's under handed tactics and its pursuit of the unwitting:

> Clayton's predatory practices have damaged minority communities
> — from rural black enclaves in the Louisiana Delta, across
> Spanish-speaking swaths of Texas, to Native American
> reservations in the Southwest. Many customers end up losing their
> homes, thousands of dollars in down payments, or even land they'd
> owned outright. (Baker & Wagner, 2016).

In other words, what Buffett is doing in Omaha, Nebraska with his new "75 North" project – building condos and housing in the heart of the black community that only he and Susie can control – is nothing new. Take note of the previous areas of exploitation: the Louisiana Delta, Latino areas in Texas and reservations in the Southwest, probably Arizona and New Mexico.

Mobile homes mean low-income and low income people are rife for exploiting. Take note of the following factoid:

> Over the 12 years since Buffett's Berkshire Hathaway bought
> Clayton Homes Inc., the company has grown to dominate virtually
> every aspect of America's mobile-home industry. It builds nearly
> half the new manufactured homes sold in this country every year,
> making it the most prolific U.S. homebuilder of any type. It sells
> them through a network of more than 1,600 dealerships. And it
> finances more mobile-home loans than any other lender by a factor
> of more than seven. (Baker & Wagner, 2016).

The key to the previous information lies in the term "mobile home loans." So Buffett's people are working with lending interests to provide low income housing and then collects on the rents as well. In other words, he has cornered the market. And it's more evident when it comes to communities of color:

> In minority communities, Clayton's grip on the lending market
> verges on monopolistic: Last year, according to federal data,
> Clayton made 72 percent of the loans to black people who financed
> mobile homes. The company's in-house lender, Vanderbilt
> Mortgage, charges minority borrowers substantially higher rates,
> on average, than their white counterparts. In fact, federal data
> shows that Vanderbilt typically charges black people who make
> over $75,000 a year slightly more than white people who make
> only $35,000. (Baker & Wagner, 2016).

Let's look at the data and see how it can potentially be juxtaposed with what Buffett is doing in and to the black community of Omaha.

First, the fact that his company, Clayton, made 72 percent of the loans to black people who financed mobile homes. The interest charged must be astronomical, the way it usually is when white people deal with minorities. So all of that is profit and it is funneled upstairs to Buffett's holdings. So when he boasts about giving away part of his fortune or donates a mobile home to an elderly woman the way his sister Doris did, he's talking out of his ass. He is so greedy that to make such donations is nothing more than chump change for him.

Secondly, minorities get charged "substantially higher rates, on average. As stated earlier, people of color are always going to be treated like a pariah group, even when there is a business transaction. So again, all people of color represent to the Buffetts – especially Warren and Susie – is a profit margin. They will hunker down and bring on people who have similarly racist tendencies to serve as "front men" for their various enterprises, build or construct housing or nonprofit institutions, and as Warren himself said, he doesn't believe in contributions or donations – only "investments." Black people are a commodity – seen either as a tangible asset (renter, client) or a crippling liability (their mere existence).

Third, the statement that Clayton's grip on the lending market in this area verges on the monopolistic. A monopoly is more than just majority control of something. A monopoly is defined as, "Market situation where one producer … controls supply of a good or service, and were the entry of new producers is prevented or is highly restricted." (BusinessDictionary.com, 2017).And here is what we need to realize and understand.

The idea of being able to prevent the entry of new producers or competition is a key when it comes to such monopolies. In Buffett's case, he can dominate the mobile home loan market and the companies that make those homes, by extension. By controlling the companies that make the homes, that means that he has some say in how those houses are made and more likely than not, their destination and quality. He controls the hiring process, which means more likely than not he is going to bring on cheap labor and use cheap materials which will enable those homes to be mass produced. This all goes into monopoly capital and the more you learn about it, the more you can see how grotesque and greedy Buffett is and how vulturistic his holdings are.

Like the cowardly Trump, Buffett only approves of answering questions and talking to the media when he is making announcement or being interviewed for another "fluff piece" article. In other cases, check out his actions:

> Through a spokeswoman earlier this month, Buffett declined to discuss racial issues at Clayton Homes, and a reporter who attempted to contact him at his home was turned away by security. Clayton and Berkshire Hathaway did not respond to numerous

> requests for interviews with executives, delivered by phone and email, as well as in person at Berkshire Hathaway's headquarters in Omaha. The companies did not answer any of 34 detailed questions about Clayton and its practices. Nor did they respond to an extensive summary of this article's findings, provided along with an invitation to comment. On its website, Clayton says that it seeks to "treat people right" and "preserve our integrity above all else." (Baker & Wagner, 2016).

You can see how Buffett is shielded by his security staff and even by the local media. He did not respond to the questions because he knew that just the fact that the questions were being posed showed that the people asking the questions KNEW something. And obscurity and secrecy is a key to Buffett being able to hide his perfidious and perversely parasitic activities. To the Omaha hick and others, he's just a good ol' rich white man; but this short book exposes it in a way that few, if any, have ever done before.

Look at where the Clayton website claims that it "seeks to treat people right and preserve our dignity above all else." This is the typical mission statement of any white organization that wants to pimp the minority quality of life. They talk as if they don't see the racial differences, which would be an insult in and of itself. They talk as if they truly believe in the "brotherhood of man." But these peckerwoods, no matter how rich or well off, have an almost genetic hatred for anyone producing significant amounts of melanin for adequate skin coloration. They can't do it so they hate the ones who can (produce skin color).

How does he do it and what is the outcome. According to the article, "Clayton Homes, the largest U.S. builder of mobile homes, sells them through a network of more than 1,600 dealerships. It also finances more mobile-home loans than any other lender by a factor of more than seven" (Wagner, 2016). But denial is the main weapon of people like these. According to the writer of the article,

> After publication of this article, Clayton issued a news release, accusing the reporters of "activism masquerading as journalism" and stating: "We categorically and adamantly deny discriminating against customers or team members based on race or ethnicity." For two specific categories of loans, the company said, minorities pay the same or slightly lower interest rates than whites.) (Baker & Wagner, 2016.

If the Buffett-based denials sound familiar, they should. These are the same "we did nothing" and "blame the fake media" type rebuttals that you hear from the duplicitous President Donald Trump. Furthermore, if minorities pay the same or slightly lower interest rates than whites, when it comes to the latter area of paying lower interest rates, that is STILL a form of discrimination! And why would they do that? Perhaps to extend the period of the loan and in doing so increase the amount of total interest paid? A white man is not going to cut a person of color any slack unless there is a profit motive involved – a lesson that history teaches us time and time again.

The explanation of how much Clayton Homes does for minorities continues in the following passage:

> Clayton has expanded its minority customer base — 31 percent of its loans went to minorities last year, up from 22 percent in 2008 — with the help of meticulous demographic analysis and targeted sales promotions. Spanish-language ads in Texas promise Latino immigrants without Social Security numbers that they, too, can enjoy the American dream of homeownership. (Baker & Wagner, 2016).

So fudging, manipulating and breaking the law and the data in the name of minorities is the only defense they've got! Let's analyze what we just read.

If you expand your minority customer base with loans, that's creating MORE dependency on the system. That is money that has to be paid back, so you're doing yourself a service, NOT the minorities! That "meticulous demographic analysis" and "targeted sales marketing" is just business talk for "minority targeting." They hunt for minority sections in need and then send them those specialized flyers or targeted TV commercials the same way that those for profit colleges do when it comes to recruiting minority kids!

Moreover, the Spanish-speaking ads in Texas that makes those promises to Latino immigrants without social security numbers are again, doing Clayton Homes a favor – NOT the immigrants. In fact, they are helping the immigrants to break the law and it's a scam. When the immigrants get busted by the racist patrols for not having social security numbers, they are deported – and Clayton Homes can then take that same home and rent it out to someone else! All the money that was paid by the person who got deported is lost and if they return, they start all over again.

Who do these peckerwoods think they're foolin'?

Clayton Homes got caught in the scam on more than one occasion as the following excerpt implies:

> As it drew in more Latino customers, however, Clayton's practice was not to provide Spanish-speaking customers with translated loan documents or interpreters at closing — even after employees

at headquarters complained that too many customers were being
misled about loan terms. Fair-housing laws prohibit lenders from
targeting and overcharging people of color, whose communities
historically were denied access to credit. (Baker & Wagner, 2016).

But the Clayton people knew full well about the translation issues and merely exploited them – just as they do in Omaha with illiterate and nearly illiterate black people in order to get them to sign up for their bullshit programs. The Fair Housing people in Washington, DC. should be contacted about what Buffett is doing to these small minority communities and the role that various city administrations play in looking the other way while Clayton Homes, with Buffett's blessing, gets away with minority scam after minority scam.

Put another way,

Clayton's practices are part of a corporate culture that has
condoned racism, including black employees fired while white
workers used discriminatory slurs and kept their jobs, and phone
collectors casually insulting borrowers with racist stereotypes.
(Baker & Wagner, 2016).

And Warren had to know about that because he is the man who oversees everything and collects the profits. He hears the complaints but just as he does in Omaha, he turns a deaf ear. As I made clear elsewhere in this book, Buffett's home is located less than five miles from the largest (and only) ghetto in the entire state. And for all those years he has done nothing other than to "invest" and disguise those investments as contributions. His daughter Susie is buying up the black community lot by lot, house by house and then renting them and selling them to white people who want to return to the community and who, after all, have jobs. Remember Warren's words: he doesn't believe in contributions, he believes in investments. That is how cold this cracker is despite the hosannas of praise that are heaped upon him by leeching media types and those who want his money to promote his numerous business interests.

In the case of Clayton Homes you have a clear-cut case of exploitation, more commonly known as "predatory lending." Baker & Wagner define and explain the concept thusly:

Defining "predatory" lending
Federal regulators define a predatory loan as one that imposes
unfair and abusive loan terms on a borrower. Making unaffordable
loans based on the assets of the borrower rather than on the
borrower's ability to repay an obligation. Charging excessive
interest rates that may involve steering a borrower to a higher-cost

loan. Engaging in deception to conceal the true nature of the loan obligation from an unsuspecting or unsophisticated borrower. (Baker & Wagner, 2016).

What the previous definition doesn't mention is that those predatory loans are aimed at the poor and minority. Anyone who does it is out to make a buck at the expense of destroying people's dreams. Those big banks that Obama bailed out – many of them were in hock because of these kinds of loans.
Who's protecting the poor against usury? Quoting Aristotle, (who supposedly said these words in 350 B.C.), Rev. Paul Clearly, in his book *The Church and Usury*, wrote:

> The most hated sort of money-making, and with the greatest reason, is usury, which makes a gain out of money itself and not from the natural use of it – for money was intended merely for exchange, not for increase at interest. And this term interest, which implies the birth of money from money, is applied to the breeding of money, because the offspring resembles the parent. Wherefore of all modes of money-making, this is the most unnatural (Cleary, 1972)

In the same book Cleary quotes from Saint Thomas Aquinas who said, "He who takes usury for a loan of money acts unjustly for he sells what does not exist. It is wrong in itself to take a price (usury) for the use of money lent, and as in the case of other offences against justice, one is bound to make restitution of his unjustly acquired money."

Unjustly acquired money. The United States, being the capitalist cesspool that it is, has somehow legitimized and justified usury approaches used by pawn shops, title lenders, paycheck advance companies and so on. And that is because those with money don't use such lending services – only the poor suffer. And as long as this is the case, the majority really doesn't care, and history shows that this is the case across the board. And this is what Warren Buffett has been doing with full knowledge of the inherent evil of his actions.

But back to the Clayton Homes case:

> For an earlier story in this series that detailed Clayton's widespread abuse of borrowers, a Clayton spokeswoman said in a statement that the company helps customers find homes within their budgets and has a "purpose of opening doors to a better life, one home at a time." Buffett later defended the company, telling Berkshire Hathaway shareholders he "makes no apologies whatsoever about Clayton's lending terms." (Baker & Wagner, 2016).

Of course Buffett makes no apologies. He is about "investing," not "contributing," remember? That is the family motto. They are capitalist vampires, not Good Samaritans! The point being made in this book is that Buffett is not the "saint" that the corporate world and others seem to want to make of him. He makes these grandiose "announcements" about giving away his money but as you can see, it's nothing but a bullshit public relations ploy.

Continuing:

> For this story, The Seattle Times and BuzzFeed News analyzed hundreds of internal company documents, thousands of legal and regulatory filings, more than 40 hours of internal company audio recordings and federal data on hundreds of thousands of mobile-home loans over a decade. Reporters conducted interviews with more than 280 customers, employees and experts, including some Clayton insiders who said they were appalled by the company's practices. (Baker & Wagner, 2016).

More than 280 customers. This is no "random sample." This is a major scam that is being run by Buffett on his watch. And Omaha decides to defend him because they have to know about it. But his billions are the only thing that Omaha is really known for, so they cannot and will not bite the hand that literally feeds. All it is being done in the name of profit:

> Meanwhile, in the first nine months of this year, Clayton generated more than half a billion dollars in profit, up 28 percent from the same period last year. "It's a perpetual system of people who are never able to get themselves out of the hole," said Gwen Schablik, who worked as a collector and handled borrowers' bankruptcies at Clayton's Maryville, Tenn., headquarters from 2011 until she quit in 2014. "I felt, ethically, I couldn't continue working there," she said. (Baker & Wagner, 2016).

Half a billion dollars in profits? And the money is coming from renting out housing, mobile homes, to the poor? This spells exploitation plain and simple. Buffett cannot feign ignorance on this one; he's been informed and he knows the source and the motivations. He knows how much there is to be made and therefore he continues increasing his shares of these mobile homes. He holds a virtual monopoly, so all he has to do is find some marketing experts and promoters to publicize what he (Buffett) has to offer. He is, to put it mildly, a poverty pimp. The "oracle of Omaha" is, in reality, a "racist from the River City."

Additional evidence follows:

A culture of racism
David Ashley's problems at Clayton began soon after he became one of the few black employees to serve in management. One of Ashley's subordinates called him a "coon," and he fired her, he said. To his dismay, a regional manager overruled the decision and warned Ashley not to be so hasty, he said. Ashley said his bosses grew eager to push him out of his role managing a Clayton lot in Arkansas, even suggesting he had taken some furniture that various employees brought in and out of the lot for staging homes — an accusation that another black manager in the region reported facing around the same time. Both denied taking any furniture. When they offered Ashley a transfer to a sales lot far from his home, he said, he declined and eventually left his job in December 2012. (Baker & Wagner, 2016).

Several points to be made here.

First, note that Ashley was one of the "few black employees to serve in management." He was working around racists but he was the kind of "coon" that people like Buffett prefer and truly enjoy being around. So caught up in being "treated like an American," negroes like that can't see the forest for the trees. And they care not about how many people of color are being screwed by this old peckerwood; they just want to BELONG. And the same can be said for the backwards lot of negroes who are working for Buffett's daughter here in Omaha: a worthless lot of "prospectors" who seek out land and housing in the black community for Susie to buy up and when not doing that, pretending that they have true leadership skills.

Secondly, it is clear that others in managerial positions agreed with the subordinates referring to Ashley as a "coon. Of course they did because his actions proved that he was, indeed, exactly that. Don't you think that the roles played by Stepin Fetchit, Mantan Moreland and Willie Best were roles written by whites who were laying out a "type" of negro that they wanted projected up on that screen? The same is true in real life: job announcements go out and if the Federal government is looking then they HAVE to interview and hire somebody of color. So they make sure that the person hired is so backwards, so self-negating, so fucked up in the head that indeed, if you call him a "coon" he'll smile and learn to LIKE IT.

Third, and related to the second point is the fact that in order to call someone who outranks you a "coon," you must not have much respect for that individual. So what we have is another powerless negro who has a title and a bunch of keys that don't fit anything. Race trumps rank. In the military back in the day black men who were sergeants were cussed out and got their asses kicked by white boys who were lower in rank. In corporate America and department supervisor or the manager is often outvoted by the white underlings. When white people see race they automatically see an "inferior" and assume the inferior realizes that. It is clear that Ashley certainly did.

Fourth, the accusation of theft, which is an extension of the "coon" stereotype, since all negroes are thought to be sneaky and committed to stealing. And since Ashley was not the only black manager who was accused of theft, it is clear that the racism was focused and targeted. All of this was taking place on the beat of an organization generating big money for Buffett, meaning that Buffett was informed and kept abreast of everything, good or bad, that was taking place. In other words he knew, but didn't do a damn thing. The recalcitrance that whites show to and displayed toward black people, stereotypes of "theft" included, hail back centuries to the days of enslavement when the original "master-slave" relationship was etched in ideological stone.

Fifth the desired goal was achieved: getting Ashley out of the area and as far away as possible. If he had agreed, then these white boys can further sabotage him because by having to drive a greater distance, they can arrange for their police contacts to harass him on the road, nearby eateries to identify him and give him a hard time and more importantly, isolate him from any other black people that he might be able to unify with. It is clear that Buffett knew what was taking place. This is how a bureaucracy works, and the top dog is always kept in the loop. Meanwhile, the Omaha World Herald and the entire state of Nebraska kisses this old bastard's ass and shields him and the cornhusker public from the racism of the River City racist.

Buffett's exploitation of minorities isn't just aimed at the low-income blacks of Omaha, however. Check out the following insights provided by Baker & Wagner (2016) where they write under a sub-heading, "The Mobile-Home Trap": "Billionaire philanthropist Warren Buffett controls a mobile-home empire that promises low-income borrowers affordable houses. But all too often, it traps those owners in high-interest loans and rapidly depreciating homes." Pure capitalist exploitation by the so-called "Oracle of Omaha."

But it gets worse:

> After one of those firings in South Carolina in 2010, the company hired another black salesman. But that man, Larry Summers, testified in court records that Clayton's workers, despite his many requests, did not train him. He also said that he witnessed a co-worker make racist comments and that black customers were treated with contempt. "When I was there, I saw they treated black

customers differently than what they did white customers, you know?" he said in a deposition. "With their white customers, they're more pleasant." He said he soon quit Clayton. (Baker & Wagner, 2016).

You don't think that Buffett knows about this state of affairs? You don't think that Buffett knows about the racism that permeates his home town of Omaha, Nebraska? You don't think that Buffett listens to the admonishments of State Senator Ernie Chambers or reads my regular essays in the Omaha Star (the only contact he has with black people in Omaha)? Of course he does. The fact of the matter is simple: he doesn't give a damn. As long as he makes money, he could care less about any social obligations, penalties or stigma.

So why hire a black salesman? Because they are catering to people of color for clients. We tend to trust other "colored" people and white salesmen are more committed to their whiteness than they are to any sales pitch – and it comes across that way in their interactions. Black people should grow up and stop expecting to be treated "the same" was white people get treated. Unless they (blacks) start kicking that ass and making it clear that they are not going to be maltreated, then the first option of any peckerwood is to deride and degrade a customer of color. The record speaks for itself.

It's not just Mexico and the colored people in the mobile homes there. Check out the following:

> In Baton Rouge, La., Clayton managers engaged in "malicious and reckless conduct" by allowing employees to harass and fire the store's only black salesman, according to a lawsuit filed by the federal government against the company in 2007. A regional manager knew about the harassment, four former employees, including the victim, Melvin McNeal, said in interviews. McNeal said he complained about being called "Sambo" and "Buckwheat," but managers defended his colleagues, saying they were "having fun" with him. Two of McNeal's white co-workers backed up his complaints to managers, according to legal filings. They, too, reported being fired. (Baker & Wagner, 2016).

Another black "salesman." White people don't hire blacks to sell to white people. These are what Dr. Harry Edwards would have referred to as "niggerologists." These people are hired to go into low income areas or any area where there is a group of ignorant people who have jobs that can be convinced to "buy in" to whatever is being sold. In this case, it's mobile homes.

These are old school peckerwoods leveling names like "Sambo" and "Buckwheat." And the atmosphere was so toxic that even the white people who vouched for him got canned. But the key is that these white people heard the name calling and on their own, did NOT file any reports or concerns. Buffett is therefore guilty of knowing about these toxic and racist environments, exploiting them to the hilt and then standing back and collecting the revenue while the locals "fight it out."

And toxic it was. Check it out:

> "I can't help myself, I hate n——s," McNeal's main harasser told a contractor on the sales lot, according to a separate lawsuit filed by the two white co-workers. One remembered the harasser calling the sales lot "n——ville" when black customers arrived to tour homes. The suit by the two white employees was dismissed for procedural reasons. Clayton settled the federal lawsuit, brought by the Equal Employment Opportunity Commission, in part by agreeing to end racial harassment. The company did not admit or deny wrongdoing. (Baker & Wagner, 2016).

The agreement while admitting no wrongdoing is a part of the weakness of any of the Employment Opportunity Commission's around the country. Even if you win, you lose: the white man pays you off and then continues his doggish ways and the Commission gets to claim that they put in work, conducted an investigation and keep their jobs.

But the point to be made here is that it was a Federal lawsuit, and Buffett has Federal contracts. He had to pay up or risk losing future contracts. All the while the Omaha media is covering all this up, keeping this old racist's business dealings out of the newspaper and off the airwaves.

This article by Seattle Times reporters Baker & Wagner has a sub-section titled "steering customers" as we now move to another group, First Nation people, and a new locale, New Mexico.

Here is what they share with their readers:

> Laws designed to protect consumers prohibit mobile-home sales reps from doing double duty as loan officers unless they obtain a separate license. They can sell the mobile home, but they may not guide buyers to a particular financing option. Peter Shaw, who manages Clayton's lot in Gallup, N.M., denied that his employees steer Navajo buyers to Vanderbilt loans. He is "100 percent" sure it doesn't happen, he said, because the company trains its workers that doing so would be "strictly against the law." Yet in three dozen interviews, Clayton's minority customers said they were led

> to believe that Vanderbilt was the only option to finance their homes. (Baker & Wagner, 2016).

It's another form of "interlocking directorates" where these white people work hand in hand to funnel customers/clients to their pals in other areas of the business and then share the proceeds between them. This has been going on for centuries in America and no one said anything because the people doing it were white. Even when the laws were passed they weren't enforced because the white folks running the scam were earning money, paying taxes, employing their fellow white folks and not making any waves. When all is said and done, this is how the system works.

These First Nation people didn't have a chance. They trusted that they were in good hands and they believed that they were going to get a chance at a better life. Because of these two mis-calculations, the same thing happened to them that happened to them when they trusted the white man with what they now know as "the trail of broken treaties." Even their own people teach, "The white man speak with forked tongue."

And so the scam was launched and it was clear that poor people were being taken advantage of. Buffett was behind it all. The site was Gallup, New Mexico and the victims were people of color. Continuing:

> One of the Navajo women at the Gallup lot recorded audio of their shopping experience, including the exchange in which a sales agent told them Vanderbilt was the only financing option on the reservation. Even after being told of the recording and its contents, Shaw insisted that his employees follow the law. The company's in-house lender, Vanderbilt Mortgage, charges minority borrowers substantially higher rates, on average, than their white counterparts. In fact, federal data shows Vanderbilt typically charges black people who make more than $75,000 a year slightly more than white people who make only $35,000. (Baker & Wagner, 2016).

Keep in mind that the name of the article from the Seattle Times (a quality newspaper, unlike the Buffett controlled Omaha World Herald) is, "Minorities Exploited by Warren Buffett's Mobile-Home Empire." So what do we find?

We find a "system." This is what Buffett's Berkshire Hathaway empire is when all is said and done. I have studied systems as a sociologist and I know what the function of them is. In this particular instance, note the hierarchy of abuse where one phase/element reinforces the other: sales agent "informs" naïve minority women; sales agent convince potential clients that they are the only game in town;

the reservation is a closed system, akin to the ghetto or el barrio and is therefore a "market" that is ripe for the pluckin'; in a close system you have little contact with the outside world and therefore cannot compare what you are being charged with what those in the out-group (whites) are being charged. The system, from the sales person to the disparate pricing to the revenue stream created as a result of all of this, constitutes a pro-white "system".

There really is no way out when the "other side" is white. Even the "good ones" are nevertheless racist and it becomes a case of choosing between the lesser of two evils as far as I'm concerned. As the Seattle Times article explains it,

> In fact, there is a range of options for financing mobile-home purchases on the reservation. Many lenders make loans under a federal program created in 1992 to improve Native Americans' access to home financing. Known as the 184 Program, the subsidy guarantees that banks won't lose money on the loans. This allows them to offer interest rates comparable to a prime home mortgage. (Baker & Wagner, 2016).

Sounds like a viable alternative, right? This is another business ploy known as product disparagement. Although it is not direct in the paragraph above, it takes place when one business spreads lies about another. In this case, these "options for financing mobile-homes" are all full of shit because the concept of a mobile-home is in itself a socioeconomic boondoggle in my view. The Natives had few options and none within their "in-group" and once the trust factor kicked in, they were easy to dupe and mis-lead.

The article claims that the Navajos have their own system:

> The Navajo Nation itself also offers loans to finance mobile homes. Louise Johnson, the head of Navajo Nation's credit-services division, said tribal leaders developed the program after seeing widespread repossessions of mobile homes on the reservation. Her division offers mobile-home loans with an interest rate often under 6.5 percent — half the rate paid by many Clayton borrowers. Yet few Navajo buyers end up borrowing from the tribe. (Baker & Wagner, 2016).

So a proactive and reactive economic formulation was developed by the Navajos as an alternative. But remember what I said earlier: the choice of the lesser of two evils. Even if the Natives tried to do what was right, they were nevertheless involved in a "racket." The concept of the mobile-home is the problem and the cost, while reduced from what whitey was charging, was still as yet based on generating some semblance of a profit. So it's like what the civil rights movement did to black people: it turned us into white people in blackface, and this can be seen even in the business realm.

Here's the problem: we enter this market, like most, at the tertiary level of the economy. In other words, we buy, rent or get involved in goods and services that have already been produced. The primary sector is where products are made, grown and developed. The secondary sector is where products are farmed, harvested, manufactured. If we're not involved in either of these two, then we are simply consumers, and all we do is spend money on other people's stuff.

The key is doing for self as we did in the South and as the Natives did before the white man came and stole their land and culture. As consumers the Natives didn't stand a chance no matter how much the petitioned, picketed or prayed in public. The same thing happened to black folks.

Now, continuing, and Buffett himself now enters the picture:

> When he defended Clayton's compliance with the law earlier this year, Buffett said the company's lots use "lender boards" on their walls to show buyers the array of finance options to choose from. But the lender board at the Gallup lot, just five miles from tribal territory, had no information about Navajo credit services. It did list a lender that participates in the federal program. In an interview, however, Shaw dismissed the program as a poor option for many borrowers. (Baker & Wagner, 2016).

Just as I said earlier: "a poor option for many borrowers." Many of those people cannot read and speak a different language. Many are lacking in the sophistication needed to understand the most rudimentary concepts. It's like teaching a course in calculus to a room full of kindergartners and then telling the parents that they should be proud because the children are in an advanced class. Of what use is that class if there is no understanding of the information that is being shared or imparted?

Buffett is a racist and a con artist, just like his father was and just like his sister, Doris. And his daughter Susie is also learning the "art of the steal," as I call it. Like Trump, they have little if any regard for poor people other than as a ready-made market rife for exploitation. To Buffett and those of his ilk, minorities are just another revenue stream.

As for that "lender board," here's what it looks like and here's what it does:

> The lender board also has a single large red button labeled, "PUSH ME." By law, Clayton sales agents aren't allowed to pitch for Vanderbilt. But if they or a customer presses the red button, a digital recording does it for them: "Vanderbilt wants to finance

your home. Fast approval. Friendly service. And less than perfect credit accepted," a voice says. "Choose Vanderbilt!" (Baker & Wagner, 2016).

Bright colors. Attractive toys. Loud piercing noises. That is the way you treat and get the attention of children. And this was part of the plan. In a regular setting the color "red" means "stop," but that is the designation of a different (white) culture, not for First Nation people. So the inducement and enticements are in and now it's time for the sales people to actually take over:

> For years, salesmen received a bigger cut of the sales price if borrowers financed with Vanderbilt. That's no longer the case, but management has imposed new pressures. Clayton tracks each lot's "capture rate," or what percentage of its buyers borrow from Vanderbilt, internal records show. Managers receive reports that show how their capture rate ranks against other lots' and how their rate has changed over time. Last year, dozens of lots had capture rates exceeding 70 percent, the records show. (Baker & Wagner, 2016).

First of all the "capture rate" refers to more than just the lots in my view. The initial "capture rate" was when the prospective clients got duped by Vanderbilt and the rest and where therefore "caught up" and therefore "captured" in this giant scam, which included predatory lending. The point is that records were kept and maintained and there is no way that the top dog – Warren Buffett – didn't have access to those data and spread sheets and especially the profit shares. Just because the hicks in Omaha didn't know about it doesn't mean that none of it happened, because it is clear that it did. The Seattle Times is at least five times more credible than the Omaha World Herald, make no doubt about it.

And then there was the fact that sales persons had "goals" that they were to achieve. Check it out:

> Earlier this year, a Clayton retail vice president emailed fellow managers demanding that they explain why some stores fell short of their goals. "I know some of you are frustrated with your capture rates, as well as [retail lots] not hitting their commitments," Mark Morgan wrote in the email, a copy of which was obtained by The Times and BuzzFeed News. "They will never get to where we need them to be if they don't buy in. We must help get them there." (Baker & Wagner, 2016).

This is reminiscent of the Ponzi schemes run by people like Bernard Madoff. You get people to get into sales and then they dupe others into selling promising them a big profit. But in the long run everybody falls short because there are limited properties and victims to take advantage of . This internal pressure on these salesmen are passed down to low-income people who are duped into becoming clients in the name of "quality housing." And even if the client is illiterate or can't speak English, who cares?

For instance, read the following:

> **Papers not translated**
> Clayton has been especially effective at capturing minority borrowers — and not just Native Americans. In Texas, Clayton has blanketed parts of the state with ads, fliers and promotions in Spanish. One store promised to spare buyers the frustration of dealing with "Spanglish"-speaking sales agents: "Stop suffering, come to Clayton Homes in Seguin, where we will attend to you 100% in SPANISH!!!!" its website said. (Baker & Wagner, 2016).

Bilingual rip-offs – just like those title loan companies and the predatory lenders. When it comes to exploiting a group, the racist white man has no morals! He is willing to hire someone who is bilingual so that they can communicate the scam with the prospective victims … oops! I mean "clients." For Latinos, who are locked out of so many markets and real estate opportunities, to find a sign that accommodates their language issues is a welcome sign. And they enter the Clayton offices with an open mind and a warm heart and leave having been ripped off and otherwise taken advantage of.

The data does, indeed, tell the tale:

> Vanderbilt and Clayton's other lending division, 21st Mortgage, originated 53 percent of all mobile-home loans to Native Americans; 56 percent of loans to Latino and Hispanic borrowers; and 72 percent to blacks, according to 2014 federal loan data from some 7,000 lenders. Among white borrowers who were not also identified as Latino or Hispanic, Clayton's market share was 31 percent. (Baker & Wagner, 2016).

Look: all people of color. Black people are the ones who come in first place in the Buffett exploitation competition, just like they do in Omaha, Nebraska where Buffett's so-called "75 North" project is nothing more than an effort at age and racial re-segregation. But in second place are the Latinos and the Native Americans, who are barely a part of the American populace any more after near genocide by white people, still make up 53 percent of mobile home loans. That 31 percent of white homeowners were of the poor white trash ilk that you find usually living close to us because of incompetence, marriage to a person of color, or outright gooniness. This was the 21st Mortgage record, a lending division of both Vanderbilt and Clayton.

Furthermore,

> Blacks, Latinos and Native Americans tend to have lower median incomes and lower credit scores than white Americans. As a result, the loans they receive — for houses, cars or virtually anything else — often have higher interest rates. So Vanderbilt is not alone in charging minority customers more, on average, to finance their mobile homes. What sets the company apart is just how much more. (Baker & Wagner, 2016).

On the other hand,

> Clayton was less reliant on lending to minorities in 2004, the first full year after Buffett's Berkshire Hathaway bought the company for $1.7 billion. Around that time, then-marketing manager Robert Fox explained in a recent interview, Clayton was beginning to harness emerging research tools to help identify untapped markets. (Baker & Wagner, 2016).

With 21st Mortgage handling the "colored folk," Clayton was engaged in research and revenue generation. That's what "beginning to harness emerging research tools to help identify untapped markets" means. What it means is "looking for some new niggas to exploit, looking for some new weak-minded people, like single mothers, the handicapped, veterans who can't find housing and so on. Like Trump, it is clear that Warren Buffett's morality has no bottom.

"Untapped markets" means those markets rife for predatory lending. That's why the banking industry crashed a few years back – giving out loans to people that they knew would not be able to pay them back. But the white man doesn't care; he can foreclose and take the property back and re-sell it later. In the meantime he has all these people on the hook and has screwed up their credit in the meantime.

So you target weak markets and seek to find places where they are congregated and compartmentalized. Put another way,

> After analyzing its Vanderbilt loan portfolio to understand the demographics of its customers, he recalled, Clayton then searched for areas where these market segments — people with similar characteristics — were clustered. For one presentation in 2005,

> Fox mapped Houston-area ZIP codes where these potential customers lived. Four of the five market segments he highlighted were identified as ethnically mixed. "It was extremely cutting-edge for the manufactured-home industry," Fox said. (Baker & Wagner, 2016).

Complicated sounding words that still spell out the process of "ready, aim, fire!" For instance, the statement, "After analyzing its Vanderbilt loan portfolio to understand the demographics of its customers, he recalled, Clayton then searched for areas where these market segments — people with similar characteristics — were clustered." "Searched for areas"? That was easy enough to find. People with similar characteristics? Just seek out people of the same socioeconomic status, racial group or ethnic group. In other words, slums, ghettos, barrios and reservations. The term "cluster" is a fancy way of saying compartmentalized, ghettoized, crammed, batched, bundled up, etc.

Additionally, because America is segregated, locating zip code demographics is very simple. The poverty zip code in Milwaukee is 53206, in Omaha it is 68111, and Dallas has several of them. It does not take a rocket scientist to know that poverty zip codes are made up of people who are poor and are kept that way so various cities can document them as "pockets of poverty' and use those demographics for inclusion in grant applications to beg for federal money: police grants, social service grants, housing grants, special education grants and so on. This has been going on for at least a century.

Speaking of First Nation people, pay close attention to the following passage and how that "cluster" is viewed in the same way as other (racial) "clusters":

> More recently, Clayton has drawn in minority borrowers with targeted marketing, such as sponsorship of a Lumbee Tribe powwow in North Carolina. Louisiana dealerships have advertised single-parent loan programs in a state where black families are more than twice as likely as white families to be headed by a single parent. And in Texas, Clayton has blanketed parts of the state with ads, fliers and promotions in Spanish. One store promised to spare buyers the frustration of dealing with "Spanglish" speaking sales agents: "Stop suffering, come to Clayton Homes in Seguin, where we will attend to you 100% in SPANISH!!!!" its website said. (Baker & Wagner, 2016).

There you have it: a scam for the First Nation, one for Blacks and one for Latinos. How can anyone in a court of law deem this a "quirk" or an accident? These facts are the quintessential foundations for discriminatory targeting. And remember: Buffett had to know about it beforehand, during and since. He had to give the go-ahead and at one of those "committee meetings," he had to approve it.

Moving on:

> Another lot's Spanish-language ad addressed immigrants who have government tax ID numbers but no Social Security number: "No credit, no Social! Your ITIN and your promise is all we need!" But when the time came to sign a legally binding loan, the company's Spanish language skills disappeared. Its practice was to provide loan documents, full of dense legal jargon, in English, and not to provide interpreters, according to 12 Spanish-speaking borrowers who purchased homes in Texas over the past few years. (Baker & Wagner, 2016).

Every discount, every break and every "opportunity" is allowed to these low-income minority people to get them "hooked" on and into the system. These fast-talking salesmen offer the scam in bilingual terms so that the potential client can be further duped into thinking that Buffett and his cronies truly give a shit about them. Then pack the documents with legal terminology that these people, who have no attorneys with them, cannot understand. They just sign on the dotted line and before you know it they think that they have a piece of "the American Dream." But what they really have entered into is a poor man's version of "the American nightmare."

Take the case of a single mother who felt she was getting a "deal":

> That's how Rocio Orozco, a single mother living in rural Willis, Texas, who speaks only enough English to carry on a simple conversation, said she ended up paying nearly double the interest rate she was promised — and losing $500 of her down payment to her local Clayton-owned dealer before she'd even signed the contract. After driving past Clayton's dealerships on her way to work each day, Orozco, a manager at Subway sandwich shops, stopped at a Clayton-owned lot in early 2012 to "window shop," she said in an interview conducted through a translator. She said she told the sales reps that she didn't have good enough credit for a loan. Still, she recalled, the rep went to lunch with her, talked to her about their families and told her not to give up hope. (Baker & Wagner, 2016).

Ripping off people of color and taking advantage of those with language difficulties. Isn't that what kleptocrats do? Do they not mis-direct monies into their own pockets while money for upgrades, repairs or programs go unattended? Can such an attitude not also operate on the micro-level?

The white man, in general, has a long history of doing this around the world. He doesn't care as long as what he does feeds into the bottom line and generates yet another revenue stream. You just read a case where a woman comes into talk, is seduced with a free lunch, and it told not to give up hope. "Hope" is what these white people – just like ministers – feed to people who don't have any. But as the old saying teaches us, "Hope without a plan is a dream." And far too many poor people are left "dreaming," being force-fed that Martin Luther King, Jr., "I Have a Dream" bullshit and in the process of dreaming are all the more vulnerable to any sales pitch that comes their way.

But the "application process" doesn't just stop with the victim ... ooops! I mean "client" being told to "hold on." Take note of the following:

> Before Vanderbilt would process her application, Orozco recalled, she was asked for a $500 deposit, delivered on a blank money order. The loan for a double-wide came through, but the $500 disappeared. Documents indicate it was not credited against the cost of her home. In fact, the loan balance was inflated by $5,866 in fees and Clayton-brokered insurance, nearly as much as her down payment. She hadn't noticed the additional charges until a reporter pointed them out. (Baker & Wagner, 2016).

It was a ripoff from the get-go. It starts with a $500 deposit which is non-refundable. No paperwork, no contractual agreement, just a pimp-like "gimme some money, bee-och!" And she handed it over because, like the Christmas poem says, she had "visions of sugar plums" dancing sweet in her head. She sensed ownership. She sensed security. So in her view, any risk was worth hit. It's that old poverty maxim of "with high risk comes high rewards."

Furthermore, the money order was blank, meaning that the sales person who was working with her probably pocketed it as some kind of "hazard fee." That's what those white boys do. The front office tells them to "keep whatever you can get," and that serves as an incentive to the sales people to get out there in those slums and "bring us some customers!" Don't forget that most of these sales people were losers themselves. But like most preachers and ministers, they were losers blessed with the gift of gab. And what's what you need in order to talk people out of their hard-earned money.

Third, the deposit wasn't credited, as I said and the cost of the home remained the same. Not only that, but additional fees were added. Just as the sales people are given incentives in cash, the people higher up are as well. That is what the words "fee" and "service charges" come to mean in the long run. What service? The poor don't even bother to ask: they just pay and hope that they will have a tangible asset that they will be able to share with and later hand down to their children

It gets worse:

> She expressed further dismay when the reporter noted that she is paying a 14.2 annual percentage rate on the 20-year loan. The saleswoman had told her she was approved at 8 percent, Orozco said. At the loan closing, the title agent referred by Clayton rushed her through the process, showing her only the blanks on pages requiring her signature, Orozco said. (Baker & Wagner, 2016).

The key thing to remember is that Warren Buffett knows what is taking place. Somewhere along the way he has to approve these actions. Remember how elsewhere in this book he makes the statement that he doesn't make contributions – he makes "investments." But he didn't add that those investments were for himself and Berkshire Hathaway. And as you can see, he targets people of color. He is no "oracle of Omaha"; he is a "river city racist."

And poor Ms. Orozco, who never read the small print (or the large print for the most part) is left with a bunch of papers that prove nothing:

> "I said I couldn't understand them, but they told me it was all simple, just stuff the bank required," Orozco said. On the way out the door, she said, she was handed a stack of documents that she had never had a chance to review. I thought I could understand it myself, and trust them, because they were so nice. But that all changed the second I signed that paper." - Rocio Orozco Among them was a loan application, prepared by Clayton, stating that she made $4,770 a month — far more, she said, than her actual take-home salary. (Baker & Wagner, 2016).

Two points to be made here.

The first is the typical statement by these low-income people, "Because they were so nice." You can tell that the person making this statement is a female and you can also tell that in most cases the statement is made by a person of color. In the latter instance it seems that we are so desperate to curry favor with white people that if they wink or smile in our direction we act as if we've been crowned by the Lord! This is a holdover from many years of oppression and racial discrimination, and white folks know it and rarely miss an opportunity to take advantage of it.

Secondly, the inflated monthly salary on the form that she signed. So even if it was a lie put there by the company, her signature implies that she agreed with it.

So she was trapped and if she tried to renege, she would be guilty of fraud. All the company had to do was say, "that's what she told us, and see – she even signed it."

An interview with a Clayton worker appears to bear little fruit:

> Joan Norman, Orozco's saleswoman, said she couldn't imagine a case where retail workers would ask for a money order to be left blank. Norman, who no longer works for Clayton, could not explain why the $500 deposit was reflected on some documents but never applied against the cost of Orozco's home. Now facing monthly payments of about $1,000 that overwhelm her budget, Orozco said she is almost certain to lose the home. "I'm so stupid," she said. "I thought I could understand it myself, and trust them, because they were so nice. But that all changed the second I signed that paper." (Baker & Wagner, 2016).

What do you expect her to say about a blank check? It is clearly illegal! She's going to deny it and act as if she doesn't know what you're talking about. She no longer works at Clayton because she was most likely fired because she got caught and blew the whistle on the scam. Or perhaps she is just lying.

For those who think that "ignorance is bliss," merely recall the words of Ms. Orozco: ""I thought I could understand it myself, and trust them, because they were so nice. But that all changed the second I signed that paper." Lawyers are professional cheats and liars, and contracts are written in such a way that without expertise, the wording can get right past you. This woman is not alone. There are a lot of idiots out there who think that they can save a few bucks by going over contracts on their own. And it gets worse when English is not your primary language.

For instance,

> Gwen Schablik said stories like that make her blood boil. Schablik was one of a handful of Spanish speakers working in collections at Clayton back in 2012. Every week, she said, she took calls from people whose weak command of English led them to sign loan documents they couldn't understand. Schablik and another former employee said several Vanderbilt staffers had raised the issue with their superiors. Managers eventually told Schablik that there was no need to translate the documents, she said. She continued to raise concerns, writing in an email to Clayton's director of marketing that when she spoke to new borrowers "there were many things they were not made aware about during the sale." Managers and executives, she said, dismissed her concerns; she recalled one replying, "It doesn't really matter as long as we get the money." (Baker & Wagner, 2016).

No need to translate documents which are committing people to tens of thousands of dollars in payments? These are poor people who are trusting their lives over to these white folks, and look what happened. One is reminded of the old 1973 poem by the Last Poets: "How earnest you seem/how well you did learn/ How vile a reward I received in return." And that is how these Spanish-speaking people felt, of that I am sure. And the white man's edict is akin to that of what Buffett was quoted as saying earlier in this book: "I don't make contributions, I make investments." And what do you see in the previous excerpt? A similarly diabolical declaration: "It reallydoesn't matter as long as we get the money."

Need I say more? I will anyway – just to make the case against the River City Racist:

> More than a dozen Spanish-speaking borrowers in Texas said they initially dealt with friendly, Spanish-speaking retail staff, only to be rushed through loan closings that the borrowers didn't understand, conducted entirely in English. Many said they were surprised to find that the loan terms were much more costly than they'd been told. (Baker & Wagner, 2016).

Where is the reporting by the Omaha World Herald? Why do I have to read about these incidents in the Seattle Times? Each newspaper relies on the Associated Press and they pay a fee to access what they view as "important news." So that means that the World Herald editors saw these stories about Buffett (and there were scores of them) and his ripping off of Latinos and First Nation people and consciously chose not to print them. In other words, since the World Herald owns every newspaper in the state of Nebraska, by leaving out the stories of Buffett's racist behavior, they therefore shield him from unbiased scrutiny. All the hicks from Nebraska read about is how great he is and how he and his daughter are trying their "garsh-darndest" to help the negroes.

Moving on:

> In at least six states, Clayton managers have permitted open racial hostility toward people of color, according to interviews and legal filings by more than 15 former workers with direct knowledge of the incidents. For decades, until federal fair-housing laws were introduced in the 1960s, banks routinely engaged in "redlining" — literally drawing red lines on maps around minority communities where they would refuse to make loans or open branches. (Baker & Wagner, 2016).

Discrimination in at least six states. Buffett had to know what was taking place because these people report to him regularly. He reads the reports. Redlining is a strategy that Omaha should well be familiar with since it is a city that made such a tactic a way of life when black people began migrating into the city. Buffett was in Omaha at that time and what did he do? *Nada.*

Therefore,

> Clayton appears to have engaged in reverse redlining, seeking out minorities and charging them higher rates, according to a review of company documents, interviews, and an analysis of federal loan data. "Absolutely classic reverse redlining," attorney John Relman called it. The practice may violate the federal Fair Housing Act or the Equal Credit Opportunity Act, said Relman, who represented the city of Baltimore in a suit against Wells Fargo for reverse redlining. (The bank, which did not admit wrongdoing, settled, agreeing to spend millions of dollars on housing initiatives.) (In its news release after this article's publication, Clayton said that "we do not 'target' minority markets or engage in 'reverse-redlining.'") (Baker & Wagner, 2016).

If this so-called "reverse redlining" was taking place and there was evidence of it, where are the class action lawsuits? Where is the national press conference via CNN and MSNBC exposing all this? The answer is clear: Warren Buffett's mythical character of being the "Oracle of Omaha" shields him from the type of scrutiny that crimes like his truly deserve. He gets away with it because of his image as an old hick who knows how to make investments. And has made enough white people rich to be able to add additional protection to his reputation, which is why you don't hear about the "reverse redlining" and the "real estate discrimination" that I am writing about in this book.

The "targeting of minority markets" is nothing new in American business. It is known as "niche marketing" in the business classes taught at universities around the country. The existence of different types of food being distributed to different "areas" of a community, the fact that low-income and minority areas receive lower quality goods, the existence of predatory lending and similar tactics all show that there is a "targeting of minority markets" taking place.

As yet another example that may appear to be a drift from the subject but which I am using to make it clear that "targeting" in the negative takes place on a number of planes, take the case of the "expired Coca Cola" incident from 2002:

> From the shade of a loading dock, watching the big rigs shed
> payloads of leftover Coca-Cola for supermarkets in the black

neighborhoods of Dallas, William D. Wright says he learned how to keep quiet and do as he was told. For years, he says ,he stripped expired pop cans from their cardboard sheaths, stuffed them into fresh boxes with new dates stamped on the side, then piled them on store shelves as if they were new. As long as they had no leaks, dented cans were sometimes repackaged, too. It was all part of what his coworkers called the fires sale. "I knew what we were doing was not right," said Wright, who delivered Coke for 145 years. "But every time I brought it up, I'd hear: 'I'm the boss. You do what I say'" (Winter, 2002).

Doesn't this sound like the types of racist and condescending comments that the Clayton people were using against their black managers? The story continues:

Marching with bullhorns and spreading their message over talk radio, dozens of Coke drivers, plant workers and salespeople are accusing their bosses of inching up profits for almost a decade by pawning off expired pop cans and bottles on minority communities across north Texas. Rather than throw away the old drinks, the workers say, factory manages have ordered them to salvage truckloads of old, unsold drinks from stores in predominantly white areas, only to cart them to the poorest neighborhoods – where shoppers are seen as just as thirsty but a lot less discriminating. "It still looks good to the naked eye," said John Wayne Waleford, a Coke driver for the past 14 years. "But the people in the community don't know what they're buying" (Winter, 2002: 21A).

Again, similarities with the Vanderbilt and Clayton Homes racist activities and attitudes where the previous excerpt regarding Coke customers are also minorities and share similar reactions to a white product. Recall where is stated, "factory manages have ordered them to salvage truckloads of old, unsold drinks from stores in predominantly white areas, only to cart them to the poorest neighborhoods – where shoppers are seen as just as thirsty but a lot less discriminating. "It still looks good to the naked eye,"

So whether we are talking about Spanish-speaking people, Native Americans or African-Americans, "target marketing" in the negative is alive and well.

Now we go from Dallas and the Coke incident and return to nearby Louisiana:

In Louisiana, where Clayton controls 80 percent of the market for mobile-home loans to black people, the company sold Helen

> Shorts, a disabled grandmother, a loan she had virtually no chance of repaying. Shorts, who is black, said she lost her previous home to a fire in 2013, leaving her and her family with almost nothing but the clothes they were wearing. Barely able to afford food, she said, they relied on handouts from churches and slept on friends' floors. When her insurance check finally arrived early last year, Shorts recalled, she and her husband, Leroy, were desperate to turn it into permanent housing for the three grandchildren they look after. She and a girlfriend drove more than 50 miles to a Clayton sales lot in Gonzales, La., that, she said, had advertised homes for as little as $7,000. (Baker & Wagner, 2016).

A disabled grandmother who is desperate and in need. And these assholes had nary a concern about those demographics: they just wanted the money. So in a small town of Gonzales, Louisiana, Clayton Homes had an office.

I did some research on Gonzales, Louisiana, and the key demographics are these. The town is 47.6% Black meaning there are 4,915 residents. It is 44.5% white, meaning 4,597 residents. But the key is the population density. The town has a land area of 8.37 miles, meaning there are about 1,249 people per square mile. This makes that town about the same size as Omaha's black community. Clayton Homes knew what they were doing when they opened up an office there. They were taking advantage of the low income and minority and they full well knew it. This is the "minority targeting" that we addressed earlier in this book.

Now we move on to the case of Ms. Shorts:

> Shorts went into the store looking for payments of $300 to $400 a month, she said, something she could afford on her $749 in monthly disability benefits. The saleswoman, she recalled, later told her that she was lucky to qualify for a loan on a bigger, used mobile home priced at $55,000. Clayton financed it for her with a Vanderbilt loan at a 15.77 annual percentage rate, after a down payment of $7,000. When she and Leroy returned for the closing, they said that, like many other buyers, they were rushed through it. Agents quickly turned over page after page, saying, "You need to sign right here, sign here, sign here," recalled Leroy, who said he has been unable to work since he went blind in his right eye. (Baker & Wagner, 2016).

So they gave these two elderly black people the bum rush. They bamboozled them. And guess who has to know about these tactics? Warren Buffett. There is no way that such overt improprieties would and could be undertaken without the so-called "oracle of Omaha" knowing about it. So he is complicit in the scam. And yet

Omaha is turning their heads to the dirt he does because he's an old man and he says the right things at the right time.

Now, the plot thickens:

> The monthly payments were $851 — about $100 more than the amount she received from her fixed disability payments. Shorts, who said she didn't realize how much she would have to pay every month, made just two payments, then defaulted in June 2014. Clayton filed to seize the home that October. (Baker & Wagner, 2016).

Why didn't her blind husband kick something in to help with the costs? Where are the children of these old people? If they wanted the house they should have known they had to make long-term preparations to stay in it. But the real issue is that they were cheated by Clayton, who knew what the woman told them and saw the applications where she specifically stated that her max amount was just over seven hundred dollars, and yet they jacked the monthly payment up a hundred dollars more. And as soon as the elders couldn't pay, here comes Clayton ready to evict them. And it's not just a regional thing or a Clayton Homes application issue. Pay close attention to the following:

> Even when loans go bad quickly, the sale can be profitable for Berkshire Hathaway. Clayton often marks up new homes about 70 percent over invoice, company documents show. After a 20 percent down payment and thousands of dollars in fees added into the loan, Clayton can recoup more than half the wholesale price of the home in a year. When borrowers stop paying, the company can repossess and resell the home, again with another markup. (Baker & Wagner, 2016).

This is typical for the housing and real estate industry but most people aren't as obvious with their heinous actions as Clayton Homes. Buffett is involved and knows it, and yet people tend to turn away from his greed-oriented acts. As Karl Marx once wrote, "Capital is dead labor, which, vampire-like, lives only by sucking living labor, and lives the more, the more labor it sucks." Clayton Homes and Warren Buffett fit this definition like a glove.

More evidence follows. Under the sub-heading "Threats, Mockery," Baker & Wagner (2016) write,

> Arriving at Clayton's Maryville, Tenn., headquarters each morning, collections workers and their colleagues shuffle past a poster of Warren Buffett pointing to his "rule of thumb." The

> company's practice was to provide loan documents, full of dense legal jargon, in English, and not to provide interpreters, according to 12 Spanish-speaking borrowers who purchased homes in Texas over the past few years.

This is clear evidence of complicity on Buffett's part. He might argue in court that he "had no idea what was going on," but that lie would be pummeled with the types of facts that have been provided by the Seattle Times and, of course, in the analyses within this black paper. Warren Buffett, like Bernie Madoff and others, has literally gotten away with high crimes for more than six decades. And in the country that is even now boasting about its moral compass and "world leadership," here is a man who is continually featured as one of the world's richest without nary a mention of the poor and minority communities that he pimps, placates and eventually pulverizes in order to add to his already burgeoning coffers.

Continuing:

> "I want employees to ask themselves whether they are willing to have any contemplated act appear the next day on the front page of their local paper — to be read by their spouses, children and friends — with the reporting done by an informed and critical reporter," it reads."I'd pass by that and I was just, like, 'Are you kidding me?'" said Schablik, the Spanish-speaking employee who, until last year, worked as a Clayton collector and handled borrowers' bankruptcies. (Baker & Wagner, 2016).

There you have it: we have motive, method and opportunity. And to add icing to the cake we have evidence of intent. This is organized crime in its purest form. In my view what Buffett has done is a direct violation of the RICO Act – Racketeer Influenced and Corrupt Organizations. As a teacher, I am obligated to explain things to those who may not be informed, so a brief explanation of a RICO violation is in order.

According to Wikipedia,

> Under RICO, a person who has committed "at least two acts of racketeering activity" drawn from a list of 35 crimes—27 federal crimes and 8 state crimes—within a 10-year period can be charged with racketeering if such acts are related in one of four specified ways to an "enterprise" … Those found guilty of racketeering can be fined up to $25,000 and sentenced to 20 years in prison per racketeering count … In addition, the racketeer must forfeit all ill-

gotten gains and interest in any business gained through a pattern of "racketeering activity.

What has been described within the pages of this brief paper constitutes a form of racketeering. Buffett need not have laid his hands on the process, but he certainly benefited from the product. Besides that, the plans had to have his approval or none of the entities mentioned would have been able to make a single move. If it is difficult to picture Warren Buffett as a racketeer (and by now it should not be), then let's contemporize what he's done to low income and minority peoples and take note of another billionaire who bamboozled folk and was busted under the RICO statute: none other than current president Donald J. Trump.

In the case of Art Cohen vs. Donald J. Trump, the following took place in a San Diego court:

> *Art Cohen vs. Donald J. Trump* was a RICO class action suit filed October 18, 2013, accusing Donald Trump of misrepresenting Trump University "to make tens of millions of dollars" but delivering "neither Donald Trump nor a university … The case was being heard in U.S. District Court for the Southern District of California in San Diego, by Judge Gonzalo P. Curiel … It was scheduled for argument beginning November 28, 2016 … However, just 20 days before that date and shortly after Trump won the presidential election, this case and two others were settled for a total of $25 million and without any admission of wrongdoing by Trump (Conlin & Smith, 2015).

Now if what Trump did to all those students by selling them a bill of goods about getting an education – and not delivering on it and not refunding the money – then how can Buffett be any less guilty when he bilks hundreds (maybe thousands) of low income First Nation and Hispanic people out of their money and then doggishly forecloses and re-rents the mobile homes? If this isn't racketeering, then one has to wonder what is.

The case gets stronger as the following excerpt makes most clear:

> Even when managers were within earshot, white agents openly ridiculed black borrowers, mimicking stereotypical black vernacular on the phone, then referring to them as "n——s" after hanging up, Schablik and other current and former Clayton employees said. Two collectors recalled English-speaking co-workers talking to Latino borrowers, repeatedly saying, "No dinero, no casa." One collector said she overheard a colleague ask

> a black borrower if she'd spent all of her money on a hair weave.
> (Baker & Wagner, 2016).

    This is a case of overt racism. This is that KKK-type racism that these white people used to openly exhibit in the Deep South when they had free reign and the entire system behind them. This is a throwback to the days of enslavement. If the Seattle Times can find witnesses to share this information, why can't the Federal government do anything about it? Why can't Buffett act on what he's heard and tell these people to lay off? I'll tell you why: because, like the Federal government, Buffett is in it for the money and the number of revenue streams he can produce. And when those are your priorities, you don't give a damn about the rights of some brown, red or black people. This is the only way to logically explain how Buffett has been able to get away with these blatant acts of abuse for decades.

    Moving right along:

> On the Navajo reservation, a customer named Sheila Begay said Vanderbilt collection agents told her that Navajo people are "too stupid" to understand loan terms. Her stepfather, Daniel Teller, said they told him Navajos were so poor that they never have money in their pockets. A neighbor, Wallace Archer, recalled a collector asking whether his family had spent all of its money on alcohol. (Baker & Wagner, 2016).

    Maybe Ms. Begay is telling the truth and maybe she's not. But one thing is for sure: she would have no case were the Vanderbilt collection agents not assholes from the beginning. They were doing dirt so much that their discriminatory actions were considered par for the course. What she describes are vintage stereotypical statements made, not by ignorant red necks or hillbillies, but the average peckerwood. Corporate types and others who should know better view First Nation people as those who are sitting back on a milk crate sucking down a bottle of Jack Daniels or some cheap gin. These are the ones who are the descendants of the ones who put those "red savage" movies on television and called them "westerns." As a result, hundreds of thousands of American children of all races were running around the front yard playing games of "cowboys and Indians" with no one wanting to be an "Indian."

    This is a short snippet of the white man's past. And when it comes to race relations, the past is prologue. How can we NOT believe the words of Ms. Begay when what has been shared with you has been shown to take place wherever you have a low-income minority community?

    It doesn't stop there:

Sheila Begay leans against a fence protecting a water line where her three-bedroom home once stood in Chinle, Ariz. Her home was repossessed after she was injured, lost her job and couldn't make payments. (Donovan Quintero / Special to The Seattle Times) (Baker & Wagner, 2016).

The approach by Vanderbilt, Clayton Homes and the rest seems to rest on two words: "no mercy." These white people are smiling in the faces of anyone who might want to "check on the client complaints" and getting over because the people doing the checking are white themselves. Both have something in common: they both need to keep paychecks coming in, need to pay their suburban mortgages (if they lived near these First Nation folk and other people of color you can believe they wouldn't be pulling this racist bullshit) and need to send their children to school. That is the rationale in America, not only for racist activities on the job but also the cowardice of people of color who don't want to stand up and "make any waves."

What these folks don't understand is that the waves have already been made. The trigger to the "racial tsunami" is the minute a white salesman sees some semblance of skin color. After witnessing that, the stereotypical views kick in and all of a sudden the First Nation people become illiterate alcoholics, the black client (and employee) becomes a "coon," and the Latino renter is a "spic." This is going on because these white people committing these actions don't see them as criminal; and they know that behind them are the local cops, the so-called regulators, the National Guard, the Army, the Navy and most other institutional arrangements in this country where all men are supposedly created "equal."

And the excuses by these white folks, akin to the ones who would be interrogated in the Deep South by the FBI when they were lynching black people, are deemed "acceptable." For instance,

> Tim Williams, the head of one of Clayton's lending subsidiaries, 21st Mortgage, said in a brief interview that his collectors are trained to treat customers with respect. He said accusations that they demeaned borrowers were "very, very unlikely" to be true. "Believe it or not, not all customers are honest," he said. (Baker & Wagner, 2016).

There's a difference between a group of allegations being "very, very unlikely" to be true and those allegations being outright lies. Williams is paid to defend the bottom line and that includes whatever behaviors his people are responsible for. These are people who get off work and then head to the bar, far away from the areas they exploit, get drunk and laugh about the dirt they've done to people of color. To them its nothing but a non-stop party. And these same duplicitous assholes are the same ones who can shed a tear, bat an eye and look with a straight face into the eyes of regulators, judges and others who "swear up and down" that they would NEVER do the types of racist things that they've been accused of. It's par for the course and it's taught in a number of these training programs. When you're white the adage is, "the customer's always right"; when you're a person of color it's "the decision is always WHITE."

When it comes to Clayton's racist institutional abuse, the Latinos have their own axe to grind:

> At the tail end of the Mississippi Delta, southeast of New Orleans, Jennifer Encalade said she was receiving calls from Clayton's collection agents multiple times a day this summer. One afternoon, while a reporter was visiting, an agent named Jeremy called and began asking questions about her personal life, her financial status and her family. She put the call on speakerphone. Dissatisfied with her offer to send money after her next payday, Jeremy began to bat around ideas: Is there anyone she could borrow the money from? Was there anything she could pawn or sell? Why didn't she try something? As her 5-year-old son played quietly on the carpet, Jennifer asked: "What would you suggest?" "Uh, donate plasma?" Jeremy replied. "Or donate blood?" (Baker & Wagner, 2016).

This is the kind of attitude, captured over speaker phone, that these white people exhibit. As we've seen neither gender nor age makes no difference. But there is a basis for this that unfortunately is internalized by a whole lot of low income people and especially people of color. Let me briefly describe it.

I refer to it as the "I've-Got-Bills Syndrome." When you're poor and/or minority you hear it all the time. It's the universal explanation that is used to inform someone why you can't loan money, can't go on a vacation, can't use what little money you bring home from a paycheck on what you want. The idea of having "bills" is a kind of "rite of passage" in America, but when you're low income, that rite takes on an entirely different meaning and magnitude than when you have a chunk of change that represents what is called "disposable income." When you suffer from the "I've-Got-Bills Syndrome," you are attempting to show how respectful you are of the system and how committed you are to your debtors.

But this is all a one-way street. At night children are taught to pray, "forgive us our debts as we forgive our debtors," and in some cases it's, "forgive us our trespasses as we forgive those who trespass against us." But both sets of statements are bullshit because at the time you're saying these words, you are saying them to a make belief entity that doesn't pay bills or give a shit about debts. These words were put together by who knows who but appear in the King James version of the Bible, Matthew 6:9-13. And here they are:

> 9 After this manner therefore pray ye: Our Father which art in heaven, Hallowed be thy name. 10 Thy kingdom come, Thy will be done in earth, as it is in heaven. 11 Give us this day our daily bread.12 And forgive us our debts, as we forgive our debtors.
> 13 And lead us not into temptation, but deliver us from evil: For thine is the kingdom, and the power, and the glory, for ever. Amen.

And this is the basis of the "I've-Got-Bills syndrome" that I have proposed as a reason why people of color and the poor, who so intimately believe in Christianity and its offerings, can be told to "go donate blood plasma" in order to make a payment. These white people know of the innate religiosity of poor people and they see it every day with the number of churches that permeate black communities, the huge Catholic churches in Latino communities and the small "prayer meetings" held throughout low-income America. Paying one's debt becomes an homage to God!

In a sub-heading titled, "Family Legacy Taken," the article by Baker & Wagner documents the following:

> **Family legacy taken**
> In minority communities across the American South where Clayton has established dominance, the company seizes homes and land and resells them in a churn that strips individuals of their assets and communities from holding and building wealth. **On the Navajo reservation, geographically larger than the state of West Virginia,** there are fewer than 50,000 occupied housing units of any kind. Clayton has sought to seize homes at least 691 times on the reservation in the past decade, according to a review of records from eight of the Navajo Nation's 11 court districts. (Baker & Wagner, 2016 – emphasis added).

Clayton Homes is not going to stop doing what it does because Warren Buffett is not going to stop working to make money and bring profits to his white share/stakeholders. Could not such a situation and set of conditions be viewed as a form of "kleptocratic control"?

Now just as a sidebar, check out the fact that the Navajo reservation, a "target" of Clayton Homes is said to be geographically larger than the state of West Virginia. That is a state that is over 24,000 square miles in terms of land area. Clayton targets concentrated low income areas as does Buffett; there are 50,000 occupied housing units on the reservation. But here is the key: with all that available reservation land, it is clear that Clayton Homes will want more and will seek to "target" First Nation people from adjacent and contiguous states in an attempt to launch some kind of perverted, "go west young man, go west" trend that led to the genocide of First Nation people back in the 19th century.

Now, to show you the long-term nature of the scams that this ofay octogenarian (he is 87 years old as of August 30, 2017) has been running, let's go back to An article by Mike Baker of the Seattle Times shows that even in May of 2015 Buffett was still pulling the same capitalist and racist stunts in the name of profit.

In an article titled, "Buffett's Mobile-Home Business Has Most to Gain From Deregulation Plan" shows that Warren is working to push buttons and engage with those in power to do whatever it takes to expand his empire and the rules and regulations surrounding it. In fact in the on-line article I am about to quote from, there is a photo of Buffett on the porch of one of these homes and the caption reads, "Warren Buffett and Clayton Homes CEO Kevin Clayton walk out of a Clayton mobile home before the Berkshire Hathaway shareholder meeting in Nebraska earlier this month." So even as he was about to head to Omaha and meet up with his fellow peckerwoods, Buffett had the time to go slumming and check out one of his properties.

Now, the article on the role of deregulation (an approach which is widely promoted by current president and fellow capitalist exploiter Donald J. Trump) and what Buffett is getting away with:

> Warren Buffett's mobile-home business wants Congress to curtail recent consumer safeguards put in place after the financial crisis, saying a rollback is necessary to ensure that competing lenders continue to provide loans. But, in reality, the deregulation plan that recently passed the U.S. House would be a boon almost exclusively for Buffett's Clayton Homes, according to an analysis of 2013 federal loan data by The Seattle Times. Based on interest rate levels from that year, Clayton controlled 91 percent of the market segment set to be deregulated.(Baker, 2015).

Even with all that wealth this old man is still looking for every break he can get. And isn't this the definition of capitalism: The ceaseless pursuit of profit? He is too old to even want or need anything, but he just knows he wants more. His daughter Susie is the same way and can there be any doubt that Doris shares that same "vulturistic" gene? Back in the day the concept of "vulturistic investing" simply met buying up companies that had gone bankrupt; but when I use it as it applies to Warren Buffett and those who work with and for him, I am talking about the characteristics of an actual vulture: behavior rooted in outright greed and profit by any means necessary.

The problem is known but no one seems to want to follow through on doing anything about it. For instance,

> U.S. Rep. Maxine Waters, D-Calif., the lead congressional critic of the proposed deregulation, gave an exasperated chuckle last week when a reporter told her the 91 percent figure. "There's something wrong with legislation that would benefit any one company," said Waters, who didn't realize the proposal would serve Clayton to such a large degree. Once open to changes pushed by the mobile-home industry, the congresswoman said she has grown wary of its practices and that perhaps a federal agency like the Consumer Financial Protection Bureau should be investigating Clayton. A Senate committee is scheduled to take up the House plan on Thursday. (Bakere, 2015).

A word about Maxine Waters. This is a woman who jumps on the bandwagon of any issue that will get her in front of a camera. I will never forgive her for coming down against black rap groups and working to deny their first amendment rights just because they used words that were considered obscene. In my view her very existence is obscene. And here's something else: if Hillary Clinton didn't want to pursue Buffett because he became a major contributor to her campaign, then Waters wasn't going to do it because she and Hillary are as thick as thieves. This is 2017: have you heard anything from Waters about the deregulation issue since 2015? Of course not.

Furthermore, what were the findings of that Senate Committee that was formed after Waters became "wary" of what was going on in the mobile home industry? After all, what was going on was pointing directly at Buffett. I have heard nary a word from Waters about Buffett, Berkshire Hathaway or the monopoly of both over the mobile home business. She talks about that "perhaps" a Federal agency should be investigating: why doesn't she demand or require that an agency do it? What is this "perhaps" bullshit? Is she just watching her ass while covering for a Hillary backer at the same time?

Again, let me explain what Clayton is getting way with. As Baker once again explains it,

> Clayton's loans are particularly expensive compared with those of its peers. A recent investigation published by The Times and the Center for Public Integrity showed how the company locks buyers in loans at interest rates that can exceed 15 percent. The nation's largest manufacturer of mobile homes, Clayton sells them at its

> own retail lots, finances purchases through its own subsidiaries and
> sells property insurance on them. (Baker, 2015).

How can this not be a perfect scenario or at very least a basis for violation of a RICO statute? How are these actions not prototypical of a form of "organized crime"? People who actually worked for and at Clayton testified to the designed and intentional misfeasant activities they were getting away with:

> Buyers have described how Clayton retail outlets misled them to
> take on unaffordable loans and steered them to Clayton-owned
> lenders, Vanderbilt Mortgage and 21st Mortgage, without
> disclosing the corporate relationships. Former dealers also told of
> how Clayton Homes pressured or provided incentives to retail
> outlets to get buyers into Clayton loans. (Baker, 2015).

And the key in all of this is Warren Buffett. Congress will go through the motions, but will remain too gutless to take any steps. Why? Because the constituency involved does not carry enough political weight. And if this is the way it was under Barack Obama who is deemed "humane" when compared with most presidents, can there be any doubt that the rapacious, racist and reckless Donald Trump is not going to do anything about it?

75 North in North Omaha, Nebraska: African-Americans

The lies and half-truths that permeate the internet, most of them placed there by a group calling itself the Seventy Five North Redevelopment Corporation, clearly show that what befell the First Nation and Hispanic folk in other parts of the country was slowly but surely materializing in the Midwest as well, right in Omaha, Nebraska – birthplace of the River City Racist, Warren Edward Buffett.

I have lived in Omaha, on and off, since 1977. I am active in the community and the Buffetts well know of my battles with the police, the school system and their incursions into my community, the North Omaha area. With that having been made clear, along with the fact that I have more college degrees than any of them, I am going to use their own approved claims about this 75 North project and show the gap between the world of reality and the world of racist rhetoric, the latter being the playground of Buffett and his 75 North coterie

The website article begins with the sub-title, "How It All Began." So let's check it out:

HOW IT ALL BEGAN

> For more than a decade numerous surveys, studies, meetings and
> other community engagement activities have been conducted with
> members of the Omaha community. This extensive research
> provided a fairly comprehensive understanding of the strengths,
> weaknesses and opportunities that exist in Omaha's north side.
> (Seventy Five North Redevelopment Corporation, 2017).

When white people say "Omaha community," they mean the white power brokers. They mean suburbanites, city planners and developers all who stand to financially benefit from any pimp-type project that is being levied against North Omaha, the state's largest and only black community. So when the website makes the claim that, "This extensive research provided a fairly comprehensive understanding of the strengths, weaknesses and opportunities that exist in Omaha's north side," they mean that white people have found a way to dig in, make some behind closed door deals and once again invade the black community with programs that will generate new revenue streams for the investors who otherwise would not give North Omaha the time of day.

Of course this is not really "how it all began." The first phase was a divide and conquer tactic aimed at dissecting black voting potential. This started in the early 1980s with the North Freeway, which cut the community in half. Next came the destruction of three major housing projects, all of which were in the path that the 75 North project is now digging up and building upon. With this having been done, one need only pass by the construction site and see that white men are working in a black area, an area with the highest unemployment rate in the state. Therefore, "how it all began" was with a blatant disregard for black people and the black community, a total buying off of what little black leadership there is (with the exception of State Senator Ernie Chambers) and the complicity of black ministers and other civic types.

How it all began was with the end result being a "return to the riverfront," which North Omaha is contiguous to. But white people don't want to see black people during their Sunday cruises to the river front and to another area necessity, the Gene Eppley Airfield. So a relocation strategy begins with taking the people who lived in those housing projects and the housing that aligned the area that the North Freeway tore into and placing them to the northwest of the area that was once known as "the street of dreams." Today, thanks to the city and some negro leaders, the area is known as "the urban village." You do the math.

With that clearly understood, we now go back to the lies posted on the 75 North website:

> While a lot of great research, ideas and intentions surfaced through these studies, no concerted action had yet been taken. Meanwhile, neighborhoods were continuing to deteriorate; neighbors were becoming disillusioned; Omaha was missing out on what could be. And no organization existed with the sole purpose of implementing these findings and strategies. (Seventy Five North Redevelopment Corporation, 2017)

First, unnamed and undocumented "extensive research." And now the uses of terms like "a lot of" appear. But these nebulous descriptions are only support mechanisms for the outright lies that appear in the previous excerpt. Let me point some of them out to you.

These Omaha white people are among some of the most devilish that you will find. Not as overtly racist as in the Deep South, but a more cowardly kind of racism and discrimination. They bask in half truths – like this one, where they appear to seek to absolve themselves of all wrong doing when it comes to their gradual invasion of the black community. The site claims, "Meanwhile, neighborhoods were continuing to deteriorate; neighbors were becoming disillusioned; Omaha was missing out on what could be."

All of what is stated was by design. Neighborhood deterioration set in when, even as the city's planners admitted, they tore down too many houses too fast. Secondly, before that, when white flight took place and the whites headed to suburbia, the city services followed them, leaving North Omaha too weak to do anything but wander. The neighbors "became disillusioned" by the white site doesn't cite the reason: the reason is because black people got tired of being lied to by people who were making decisions that worked in favor of downtown and the suburbs and worked against North Omaha.

Finally the claim that "Omaha was missing out on what could be." And whose fault would that be, if it were true? What "could be" couldn't be done as long as there were 50,000 black people in the area that these white people wanted to re-take. So a gradual relocation campaign was put into effect as I've alluded to earlier. Slowly but surely the area became scattered with only the poorest of the poor left behind so that the city could continue to have a "pocket of poverty" that it could exploit in its on-going leeching for Federal grant money (Community Development Block Grants). These are the facts that the website seems to have overlooked.

Continuing:

> We felt that a single-mindedness of mission was critical to the success of any redevelopment effort in North Omaha. Given the

> stubborn nature of generational poverty and neighborhood decline, this project couldn't be an offshoot of an existing organization designed to serve a variety of needs. This project had to be the reason the organization existed in the first place. And so, 75 North was born. Borrowing heavily from the model pioneered by Purpose Built Communities, we created a nonprofit – yes, a 501(c)(3) – as an entity to drive the redevelopment of the Highlander neighborhood on the near north side of Omaha, Nebraska. (Seventy Five North Redevelopment Corporation, 2017)

Let's deal with the previous claims, and acquire a more profound understanding of how the oppressor blames the victim and how the circumstances that the oppressor initiates, all revenue oriented, are hailed as some kind of "I'll-save-you" type "solution" to the problems created by said oppressor.

They claim that there was a need for a "single-mindedness of purpose." There always has been – but not the kind that they are claiming. The single-mindedness of purpose was based on the location of North Omaha. These white cowards ran from the area during the days of white flight. They abandoned the inner city and black people moved in and made a life for themselves, including a great main north-south artery that was known as "the street of dreams." North Omaha brought more culture to Omaha than any other part of the city and the white folks saw it.

But that wasn't all. The single-mindedness of purpose, linked to location, was the need to relocate the folks who were in the area and transfer the children of those white people who fled earlier back into the inner city area. That is where the abuse of Federal funding came in. These white people, behind a major freeway, destruction of low income housing and absentee slumlords, began to manipulate the geographic configuration of the ghetto, while keeping the negative demographics (crime, drug abuse, low median housing value, high unemployment rate) intact so that they would be able to continue qualifying for that free Federal money. Single mindedness is what they call it. The rest of us would refer to it for what it was: *greed*.

Secondly, the claim is of the "stubborn nature of generational poverty and neighborhood decline." Stubborn nature? The stubborn nature belongs to the racist white people who persisted in confining black people to an 8-square mile sector of the city known as North Omaha. The stubborn nature was in the on-going leeching for poverty grants to employ fellow whites in the name of "helping the poor negroes." The stubborn nature is how these white people persist in their relocation attempts to counter-act the demographic transition that is taking place.

Third, the claim is that "we" created a nonprofit. And why was that? Because nonprofits qualify for free grant money from a number of sources, including the Federal government. Omaha's leeching has no end, and even Buffett knows where the free money can be located. Look at what he did to the First Nation people and the Latinos herein described.

Fourth, behind the veneer of "redevelopment of the Highlander neighborhood" are issues of outcomes for the rest of the area surrounding Highlander. While they claim to be about redevelopment, they are razing housing and relocating people to other parts of the city. In other words, the concept of "redevelopment" is just that, meaning "to development again." And this time around the area is going to be re-segregated, packed with people who either have good jobs or qualify for state aid and in doing so, the project generates rent for Buffett and the façade of community development. In reality, it is another way to alter the racial composition of an area and to occupy more land in the area just as they did to the Native Americans during the embryonic beginnings of the state of Nebraska's history.

The next sub-section raises the question, "Why the Highlander Neighborhood?" Following are the website's claims and my response to them.

> WHY THE HIGHLANDER NEIGHBORHOOD?
> The Highlander neighborhood was an easy choice as the first redevelopment project for 75N. Located approximately eight blocks north of CHI Health Creighton Medical Center, it is well positioned for redevelopment for several reasons. The 2009 demolition of Pleasantview Homes – a 300-unity public housing project in the Highlander neighborhood – opened up **23 acres of contiguous land less than a mile from downtown Omaha and its emerging midtown area.** It was a unique real estate opportunity with the potential for enormous community impact. (Seventy Five North Redevelopment Corporation, 2017 – emphasis added)

It's all about access to downtown with what little "leisure activity" Omaha has to offer (mainly in the Old Market) and that's where the jobs are to be found. In addition, it's about access to the airport. When white people say "unique real estate opportunity," merely recall what they did to the First Nation people and the Latinos. And then add to that the vitriol and venom that has historically been leveled against the state of Nebraska's only black community, which is where this 75 North Project is about to locate.

The excuses are ready to go, but note that no specific time frame regarding this "awareness of the problem" is ever mentioned: only vague generalities:

> The community surrounding Pleasantview homes had begun to deteriorate leaving wide swaths of vacant land and condemned homes in the Highlander neighborhood. As disconcerting as these conditions were, they also represented opportunity. It meant the **decaying housing and vacant lots surrounding Pleasantview could be acquired at reasonable prices, which would allow for development to take place at a greater scale.** By the end of 2012, 75 North owned 36 acres of contiguous land and an additional 55 lots surrounding the former Pleasantview site. (Seventy Five North Redevelopment Corporation, 2017 – emphasis added)

Look at the wording. "The community surrounding Pleasantview homes had begun to deteriorate leaving wide swaths of vacant land and condemned homes in the Highlander neighborhood." Begun when? Deteriorated due to what factors? If the City of Omaha's Department of Public Works, City Planning Department and others had been doing their job, would this "deterioration" have come into fruition? Of course not. It was all by design, and it is known as "underdevelopment" and "divestment." The sit on land and wait it out. Then they put together a bunch of developers and other (white) contractor-type groups and come up with a "plan" that they claim is going to "work for everybody."

Secondly, pay close attention to the fact that, "By the end of 2012, 75 North owned 36 acres of contiguous land and an additional 55 lots surrounding the former Pleasantview site." This means that the planning was five years in the making. But the community to be impacted didn't know about it. All they knew was that bulldozers and heavy machinery started appearing all along North 30th Street and negro leaders started singing the praises of "progress." The projects were gone and are going to be replaced by paying tenants and others who receive state aid. Any profits are going into the pockets of billionaire Warren Edward Buffett.

More lies and disguised prevarications continue on the website in the following (and final) excerpt:

> **Long standing community stakeholders have been in this neighborhood for years,** doing the type of work that could only buttress the efforts of 75 North. Strong partners and neighbors such as such as the Urban League of Nebraska, Charles Drew Health Center, and Salem Baptist Church meant the project would have a much greater chance of achieving long-term success. Highway 75 provides **quick and convenient access to major highways, downtown and the airport.** And it became the inspiration for our

> name. (Seventy Five North Redeveopment Corporation, 2017 – emphasis added)

The feckless "neighbors" mentioned are actually shills for the city. The Urban League brings nothing to the table but a hand extended seeking grant funding. The director is a former chief of police who, though black, was harder on North Omaha than a number of previous whites who held the position. Charles Drew provides health services but what do they know about community development? Their new director allowed Cox Cable to air a commercial where he said that he wanted "to be **reactionary** to the community. Not "responsive" – reactionary.

As for Salem Baptist Church, it is the largest in the community but has a long history with colluding with the powers that be. Who knows what kind of deal was cut for them to keep quiet and "allow" these white people to build a giant project less than a quarter mile from their church? Perhaps they figure that any new residents at 75 North will be a perfect "captive audience" for attending their already overcrowded Sunday service.

Conclusion: The Cover-ups Will Continue ···

Omaha will continue to worship Warren Edward Buffett as the "oracle of Omaha" and the major newspaper, the Omaha World Herald, will continue to defend Buffett and make sure no controversies surround his name. It should be mentioned that the World Herald owns almost every single newspaper in the state of Nebraska. Other than this incredible book, you will hardly find a single negative word about Buffett anywhere in Nebraska.

But is there any doubt that he is more likely to fit the description of "River City Racist"? How else to explain the abuse of low-income people in Louisiana, Hispanics and First Nation people in Gallup, New Mexico, and of course, black people in North Omaha? By their own admission his real estate people admit to "target marketing" and it is clear that the targets are people of color and poor people.

And all of these minority, low-income, politically unsophisticated pariah groups are right in the cross-hairs.

Analysis 2 –
Straight Outta Africa:

Bill Gates' "Mandela Lecture," His Vision, His Values Plans -- A Look at Modern Post-Colonial Thinking

Introduction

On October 19, 2017, when it was reported that four American soldiers were murdered in Niger. According to Starr & Cohen (2017):

> Very little has been said publicly, but the information that has emerged in the wake of the attack paints a troubling picture of what transpired. Here is what we do know: **Four US soldiers were killed and two wounded:** In what is the deadliest combat mission of Trump's short presidency to date, the Defense Department has identified all four service members killed in the ambush that occurred near the Niger-Mali border by up to 50 fighters from ISIS in the Greater Sahara, a US official said. Sgt. La David Johnson, Staff Sgt. Bryan Black, Staff Sgt. Jeremiah Johnson and Staff Sgt. Dustin Wright died as a result of the October 4 attack, after helping local forces in Niger combat terrorists.

In the first place, why would "very little be said publicly"? Why is the white man's travel and presence in and around Africa kept a secret? Why is the "deadliest combat mission" in recent years taking place in Africa and why isn't more being reported by the American (Jewish-run) media? What do they have to hide?

On October 31, 2017, Senator Tim Kaine (D-Virginia) appeared on "New Day With Chris Cuomo and Alysin Camarota. In regard to the ambush murders of the four American soldiers in Niger, he said, ""The American footprint in Africa is much bigger than the people understand." Maybe most Americans, but no all. I know the history of these white people and what they have done and continue to do to African leadership and the role they play in instigating conflicts all over the Motherland. Now we have context and the focus of this particular section of the book. Africa is the target and kleptocracy may not be Gates' goal, but he is certainly willing to take advantage of the existence of it as it exists in various African nations.

To begin with, Bill Gates is a capitalist, and the definition of capitalism is "the ceaseless pursuit of profit." And that's all he cares about. Even when he claim to be giving money away it's more of an investment than it is a donation. As you read my words you will see that Gates is committed to the same thing as all white billionaires: the maintenance of white supremacy and global imperialism with their race calling the shots.

Check out my analyses and you'll see what I mean.

Post-Colonial Thinking: Analysis

In an interview with Achille Mbembe (2008) titled, "What Is Post-Colonial Thinking?" Eurozine we have an operational definition of what most people refer to as "post-colonial thinking" but in reality, it is an extension, a modification and subterfuge for the same bullshit. Nevertheless, African scholars like Mbembe seem to think that change is a'comin'. He says, for instance,

> On the other hand, it does put its finger on two things. Firstly, it exposes both the violence inherent in a particular concept of reason, and the gulf separating European moral philosophy from its practical, political and symbolic outcomes. How indeed can the much-trumpeted faith in man be reconciled with the way in which colonized people's life, labour and world of signifiers got sacrificed so unthinkingly? That is the question Aimé Césaire poses in his *Discourse on Colonialism*, for example. (Mbembe, 2008)

What Cesaire posed was good for its time and context first of all. And secondly, it was mostly philosophical and ideological. He was basically a cultural nationalist. But he offered no real solutions to oppression by Europeans, and in my view was more committed t rebutting the likes of Shakespeare and other whites than he was in developing a rockstrong plan for black Africans.

Mbembe continues:

> Secondly, postcolonial thinking stresses humanity-in-the-making, the humanity that will emerge once the colonial figures of the inhuman and of racial difference have been swept away. This hope in the advent of a universal brotherly community is very close to Jewish thought – as projected by Ernst Bloch at least, or even Walter Benjamin – minus the politico-theological dimension. (Mbembe, 2008)

See? Even these African scholars cannot put together a plan or a paradigm unless they're kissing some white Europeans ass. That is why their thinking is so utopian and idealistic. You can't talk about post-colonial thinking in Africa because colonialism never really left – it just altered its form. That's like referring to the America of 2016 as being post-Jim Crow America when Jim Crow remains in a more subtle, covert and pervasive form. As Karenga (1967) made clear, if you are black, then your purpose is to build black. You can't talk about post-colonialism when you are mimicking and quoting the words of Europeans, people who did little or nothing to liberate Africa. People like Bill Gates, for instance.

It's easy to talk the philosophy of liberation while not actively and audaciously engaging in it. And that is what Gates is doing: talking about what all he wants to do while doing very little. Just last week on television (mid-October, 2016) he was babbling about giving away all of his money and leaving his children only about ten million each. He did not mention Africa a single time.

Along similar lines, Mbeme concludes as follows:

> That said, the postcolonial critique operates on several levels. On the one hand, like Edward Said in *Orientalism*, it deconstructs colonial prose: that is to say the mental set-up, the symbolic forms and representations underpinning the imperial project. It also unmasks the potential of this prose for falsification – in a word, the stock of falsehoods and the weight of fantasizing functions without which colonialism as a historical power-system could not have worked. In this way it reveals how what passed for European humanism manifested itself in the colonies as duplicity, double-talk and a travesty of reality. (Mbembe, 2008).

More philosophical bullshit. Just because a group is in a political state of "post-colonialism" doesn't mean that it has rejected in detail and defiance the psychological vestiges of what was left behind. Look at black people in America after enslavement: supposedly the colonial control by Southern plantation owners has ended, but look at the mental scars left behind. So once again, this guy Mbembe appears to be giving the impact of colonial control short shrift.

Secondly, he claims that the post-colonial critique, "reveals how what passed for European humanism manifested itself in the colonies as duplicity, double-talk and a travesty of reality." It didn't take a critique for anyone to see that this was the case: white people have always been viewed with disdain-and-how-dare-you; people just didn't have the guts to point it out. Europeans were fooling no one and were a joke in terms of their perpetual propensities at brutality and control and behind-the-scenes sexuality. It was no secret what these "men" and their "systems" were all about.

With these points having been made, let's take a look at the patronizing, paternalistic and patently jejune comments made by Bill Gates who, like his billionaire counter part Warren Buffett, is nothing if not a conglomeration of his own contradictions.

Contextual Appraisal: White Folks and Africa

As a long time Black Studies professor I have spent a great deal of time studying African history as it relates to the continent's long-time greatness and how the slave trade came into the picture to "under develop" the country.

I recently came across an article in Liberation News that provided an excellent capsulization of what took place after white incursion and invasion of the Motherland, tendencies that I once again see reflected in the guise of American missionaries, the World Heath Organization, the Peace Corp and other "do-gooders" who come to the continent claiming to want to "help." The kind of help that they offer is akin to what took place and comes long after the original European colonization and rape of the continent.

In order to better understand my critique and commentary regarding the "beneficence" of Bill and Melinda Gates, we must first offer a contextual appraisal of what their ancestors did. Following is an article that appeared in the October 31, 2014 issue of *Liberation News* that, though titled, "Ebola, Imperialism and Racism" nevertheless provides an excellent framework for the understanding the European and Euroamerican "obsession" with hunkering down in Africa. By also touching upon health issues, the article is again germane to the arrival of billionaires Bill and Melinda Gates and their claims of wanting to "help." My analyses will filter in and out of the article that was written by Preston Wood, a registered nurse.

The article begins, thusly:

> To understand the political dynamics of the burgeoning Ebola
> epidemic, it is necessary to see the crisis in the context of
> geopolitics and the history of colonialism and imperialism against
> Africa by the United States and Europe. (Wood, 2014).

This is the kind of contextualization that far too many studies of health and social problems on the continent are lacking in. Of course you have to view these issues within the geopolitics and history of what took place, issues that gave form and function to the problems of today. As Malcolm X said, "Of all our studies, history is best qualified to reward our research." Wood clearly understands the meaning and magnitude of Malcolm's words.

Continuing:

> The recent spotlight on the failures of the U.S. government to anticipate and prepare for a crisis such as Ebola unmasks the fundamentally racist paradigm of the U.S. capitalists towards the people of Africa. This has continued currently with racist characterizations of African people by big corporate media giants such as Newsweek, Fox News and others. (Wood, 2014).

He's talking about "U.S. capitalists" in the third person – as if he ain't one of them! This peckerwood stood by while all the things he just described took place! The "crisis of Ebola" is just one of the symptoms of the entire EuroAmerican apparatus of typing up and then raping the African continent.

And to make matter worse, he has the nerve to name names: "This has continued currently with racist characterizations of African people by big corporate media giants such as Newsweek, Fox News and others." What about those corporations he (Gates) has investments in like the Four Seasons Hotels? What about Microsoft in general?

If Gates gave a shit about Africa he would have mentioned it before coming to Africa to give a speech in South Africa in 2016. Two years before he was giving this lecture he gave an interview where he didn't mention Africa a single time. In an interview with Jeff Goodell that appeared in the March 13, 2014 issue of *Rolling Stone* magazine, check out how the interview was set up and how Gates responded, in part:

> In a substantial interview with *Rolling Stone* magazine, published in March 27, 2014 issue, Gates provided his perspective on a range of issues, such as climate change, his charitable activities, various tech companies and people involved in them, and the state of America. In response to a question about his greatest fear when he looks 50 years into the future, Gates stated: "... there'll be some really bad things that'll happen in the next 50 or 100 years, but hopefully none of them on the scale of, say, a million people that you didn't expect to die from a pandemic, or nuclear or bioterrorism." Gates also identified innovation as the "real driver of progress" and pronounced that "America's way better today than it's ever been ... Gates' days are planned for him, similar to the US President's schedule, on a minute-by-minute basis ... (Goodell, 2014).

Now remember, the previous interview in Rolling Stone was published in March of 2014 – two and a half years before the Mandela lecture. Do you see any mention of Africa? Does he even mention racism or racial issues at all? No.

When it comes to black people that is where the vague statements begin to arise. Notice where Gates says in response to a question about his greatest fear when he looks fifty years into the future: "... there'll be some really bad things that'll happen in the next 50 or 100 years, but hopefully none of them on the scale of, say, a million people that you didn't expect to die from a pandemic, or nuclear or bioterrorism." What he doesn't mention, and conveniently excludes, is the source of those pandemics, that nuclear or bioterrorism: HIS race! And because of that it is not difficult to predict! White people will blow this planet up before they even consider turning it over to black people. Gates knows that!

White folks and Africa – this is what it all boils down to. Moving on:

> In spite of recent attempts by U.S. corporate media outlets to damper down the magnitude of the ongoing Ebola crisis, it remains clear that the epidemic has taken hold and continues to expand in West Africa, particularly in Guinea, Sierra Leone and Liberia. According to the World Health Organization, there have been 13,700 officially registered cases as of the end of October, with about 5,000 deaths. Even though there is a drop in numbers in Liberia, the WHO warns this could be a temporary drop. (Wood, 2014).

White folks and Africa: Look at whose trying to indict U.S. corporate media outlets: none other than Mr. Microsoft himself. What a two-faced bastard! He talks one way in the board room and to his stakeholders and has a totally different veneer when he's speaking to a crowd of South Africans. Feigning a genuine concern, Gates continues to garble his grotesque garbage as follows:

> With a small number of infections now recorded in the U.S. and Spain, and new cases appearing in the countries in the West Africa region such as Senegal and Mali, there is no reason to conclude that the problem is simply going away. The current epidemic is by far the deadliest in history of Ebola viral infections and deaths. (Wood, 2014).

These white people can always diagnose the symptoms, but they don't want to deal with the source: THEM! White folks spread disease and they know it. That's how so many Native Americans died off after the white man came to shore. That's what led to the Black Death in Europe (although they tried to blame it on the Chinese):

> Coming out of the East, the Black Death reached the shores of Italy in the spring of 1348 unleashing a rampage of death across

> Europe unprecedented in recorded history. By the time the epidemic played itself out three years later, anywhere between 25% and 50% of Europe's population had fallen victim to the pestilence (Eyewitness to History, 2001).

The point remains that white people were weak and susceptible to the disease in the same way their diseased presence killed off thousands of natives upon their arrival to these shores.

That was another reason for the selection of Africans for enslavement. Africans had previous contact with white people and had therefore built up an immunity to them. In light of all this, any "small number of infections" that Gates now talks about may be "contained," but those who spread the disease are always going to blame the "other guy" for his/her weakness in concocting that disease.

He who controls the "tools" necessary to "fight" the disease is the one who will write the history, diagnosis and epidemiology of that disease. In the case of Ebola, the fact that it was "found" on the African continent is what serves as the subject of most international newscasts and opinions:

> A look at Ebola cases in Africa, as well as in the U.S., from a clinical/medical point of view shows that where the necessary tools are readily available to fight the disease, such as trained health care workers, including doctors, nurses, pharmacists, and so on, clinics, equipment, medications and protective measures for health care workers, and where early treatment of people who are symptomatic occurs, the mortality rates drop dramatically. (Wood, 2014).

You have to be careful about white people and their missionary-minded attempts to "help." Somewhere down the line there is money to be made. The African proverb teaches us that, "It is a wise warrior who moves with caution and discretion when an enemy throws bouquets in his direction."

When you hear about clinics, equipment and even hospitals being set up by white people on the African continent you have to first of all consider their history. Remember those "missions" that the white holy people constructed in order to supposedly "spread the word of God." Those missions became forts, armed with soldiers. Remember the "forts" that were built on America's shores? They ended up being stocked with soldiers and cannons. And the list goes on and on. Why would the white man truly want to save a people that he is genetically inferior to and sexually jealous of?

The article, "Ebola, Imperialism and Racism" continues:

> Even though the virus has been around for a long time, with
> periodic outbreaks, the world community, particularly the U.S, and
> its European allies, have done virtually nothing to prepare for the
> next time, even going so far as to drop research projects and shelve
> a promising vaccine because it did not fit into the revenue cycles of
> profit-hungry pharmaceuticals. This is criminal. The result is a
> human catastrophe that has killed thousands and portends to
> possibly soar out of control if the virus continues to cross borders
> in Africa and the world. (Wood, 2014).

There you have the truth. But most people in America are not going to read The Liberation News. They get their news from mainstream white newspapers who only give cursory attention to issues like the ones mentioned above and even then they are not about to tackle the pharmaceutical companies.

But there is an error in the previous statement where the author writes that, "The result is a human catastrophe that has killed thousands and portends to possibly soar out of control if the virus continues to cross borders in Africa and the world." If the white man has anything to do with it, Ebola and related diseases will be "contained" and limited to the African continent. These people are experts at various forms of "contagion" and they can control it if they feel that large numbers of white people are going to be effected. The best thing that Africa can provide is a ready-made pool and sample of human guinea pigs that these white people can experiment on at the ready.

And it begins and is maintained by control of resources:

> Even before the Ebola outbreak, health care in West Africa was
> weak and short on resources. Trained health care providers were
> sorely lacking. Basic infection control tools such as gloves, alcohol
> hand rubs, and soap and clean water were in short supply. Isolation
> rooms and sterilization equipment, vital to controlling infection,
> hardly existed. All these shortages still exist today. (Wood, 2014).

Next, the article touches upon what they call, "The Criminal Legacy of Imperialism," and it provides insights and information that address how the concern about "health and Africa" continues to exist to this very day in 2017.

Another little ploy that these white people like to use is to "play dumb" when it comes to looking at Africa and attempting to share with the public "just what happened." Following is an example:

> How could all this happen? A look at what Europe, and
> subsequently the United States have done to Africa over the past

> centuries clearly shows that colonialism, capitalism and imperialism have plundered and brutally exploited Africa in order to reap billions from the wealth of the continent. (Wood, 2014).

Countries don't move or act on their own. Why not come out and say "The white people of Europe and the United States"? These white people have done their dirt, raped the planet of natural and human resources, and now they want to engage in revisionist history to make it look like it was all done by some generic nation state. It was done by white people and the motivation was greed combined with racism! Say it!

Continuing:

> Having begun making inroads as early as the late 17th century, the colonial powers of Europe met secretly to make deals on how they would avoid fighting each other for the spoils of conquest by dividing up the region among themselves. This included countries such as Portugal, Germany, France, Italy and Britain. (Wood, 2014).

Still no mention of the racial motivations. No mention of the sub-human labeling of African people. No mention of the white supremacist notion that they, white people, were ordained by God to "civilize the African savages" and in doing so, were simply doing the continent a favor and were acting in accordance with Divine prophecy. When you keep facts such as these out of it, what took place sounds like a political decision based on economics. But when you tell the entire story, there should be little doubt why the continent became infected, diseased and plagued with a plethora of health problems.

The racist planning was formalized centuries ago:

> The Berlin Conference of 1884-85 produced what is called the General Act of the Berlin Conference, which amounts to the formalization outlining who among the European powers got what region of Africa to exploit and pillage. This is referred to sometimes as the "scramble for Africa." (Wood, 2014).

And there you have it: they were all involved. And the history classes in America refused to even mention or, when they did, it was a cursory statement and that was about it. The white man covered up his greed-laden crimes against Africa but still continued to act as if he was the black man's friend – just as he is doing today. And again, this was one of the reasons why so many universities feared what Black Studies was bringing to the table. When all is said and done, these

"European powers" that are even now attempting to play the role of victim were the biggest victimizers of all.

Moreover,

> The illegal and outrageous Berlin agreement led to an intensification of colonial aggression against African countries, including genocide and the destruction of towns and villages and other infrastructure, all under brutal rule. The independence and autonomy of almost all African countries was eventually overwhelmed and wiped out. Later, after World War II, the United States increased its involvement on the continent, as is well known, to become the most dominant and super-oppressive player in the region. (Wood, 2014).

So the country that promotes all this supposed "good will" is the one that eventually end up being a dominant super power. But even before that as you can see, the white folks were more committed to their whiteness than they were to any other "ism." It didn't matter if the ideology was communism, socialism or capitalism the common denominator was a blatant disrespect and hatred for Mother Africa. Today they try to deny it, which is why knowledge of one's history is of paramount importance.

> In his great book, "How Europe Underdeveloped Africa" by Walter Rodney, many important reasons for the current situation in Africa can be found. As capitalism, a system based on profits and exploitation, took hold in Europe, Rodney explains, the incentive arose for the new capitalists to further develop means of increasing profits. This meant ways to expand globally in order to find new ways and places to conquer, and then exploit the resources and labor of people around the world, including Africa. (Wood, 2014).

"Ebola, Imperialism and Racism" is an article rife with information and insights for the most part. As you can read above, a key point is lacking. He doesn't go into the role of neocolonialism, a modification from the original applications of straight out colonial control. Under neocolonialism you use people from the ranks of the people who you oppress (or at least who look like them in physical appearance) to do the bidding of the oppressor class.

Providing context is important, and Wood does a great job of it. For instance, note the following:

> Consequently, millions of African people were brutally kidnapped and sold into slavery, creating countless horrifying scenarios the

> world will never forget. Millions of others also were robbed of their wealth and forced to live miserably on their now-occupied lands under the relentless brutal yoke of colonialism and imperialism, just so the greedy invaders could enrich themselves and their class. (Wood, 2014).

All this is true. But the role of Africans themselves in that colonial system (neocolonial) also plays a major role following those kidnaps by white people. Black dictators came into power and began stealing and hording the wealth; the people starved and many were forced to flee for their lives. These realities continue to take place to this very day. I am making this punt because the speech by Bill Gates, which will analyzed later in this paper, is a part of the "new colonial" role. It is more psychological and social; it is more deceptive and financial. While what is being shared by Wood is necessary, it must be linked not only to white physicality and geopolitical attacks, but also to the psychologically manipulative interventions such as those used by people like Bill Gates and other rich outsiders.

Woods analysis continues:

> The system of capitalism, writes Rodney, in order to dominate and rule, "created its own irrationalities such as vicious white racism, and incredible poverty for the vast majority." How could Africa, with all its abundance of mineral wealth, unsurpassed history of the development of science, mathematics and analysis, be left so barren by the invading exploiters? (Wood, 2014).

I have always admired the work of Walter Rodney, but his belief that capitalism spawned racism is an area where we are in disagreement. White people were racists before they were capitalists because racism pre-dates capitalism. You can go into a socialist or communist system and if white people are at the head of it, it is racist. Racism, as accurately and astutely defined by Karenga (2010) is "an ideology, a violent imposition or an institutional arrangement." The belief system (ideology) of white supremacy and the power to impose it, along with the institutions that promote it, pre-date and transcend capitalism.

Wood then takes Rodney's incorrect assessment and arrives as his own false conclusions where he opines,

> Rodney traces the development of trade, colonial development, and imperialism as the source and cause of the extreme poverty that now can be seen in Africa, and which is so starkly seen during the current Ebola calamity …

Again, what is described above are the methods and products of white racism, not the symptoms. When those peckerwoods engaged in the development of trade, they were also engaged in cultural appropriation – the original versions of what today is called "intellectual property theft." They did it because they had no racial respect for the people who they were robbing. When they established "colonial development," they did it at the expense of people of color no matter where they went. The hierarchy was based on skin color. And as for "imperialism" as a third source and cause of extreme poverty, the fact is that racialism trumps and pre-dated poverty.

Wood quotes Rodney in the following excerpt:

> "Throughout the period that Africa has participated in the capitalist economy, two factors have brought about underdevelopment. In the first place, the wealth created by African labor and from African resources was grabbed by the capitalist countries of Europe; and in the second place, restrictions were placed upon African capacity to make the maximum use of its economic potential. "This," explains Rodney, "is why Africa has realized so little of its potential and why so much of its present wealth goes outside of the continent." (Wood, 2014).

One thing that Rodney overlooked or perhaps over-stated was obvious. He says that "Throughout the period that African has participated in the capitalist economy …." Africa was no more a participant than the mule is a participant as he pulls the plow for the farmer, who is the financial beneficiary of what is being planted! Africa was a victim and a target. Africa was a vulnerable market for the white man's lust for natural (and human) resources. You have to frame a problem of situation correctly before you can arrive at correct and accurate analyses of that situation.

Now it's back to the words of Wood who, relying on Rodney's "partially accurate" analyses, offers the following:

> This is why, also, a disastrous epidemic has begun and threatens not only Africa but the world. The solution to the Ebola crisis lays in the ability to have all the necessary equipment and trained staff to treat, isolate and contain the outbreak. Unless measures are taken by the wealthiest countries to provide the resources—supplies, medicine, organization, and health care workers—it will not be possible to bring the crisis under control. "It's only money," one might say, but the dictates of capitalism are not inclined to simply provide funds. Capitalists are generally also not willing to

> shell out funds when maximum profits are not factored into the
> equation. (Wood, 2014).

In days past the white incursion was led by the white missionary and his Bible. Today, as they seek to further encroach on the African continent, they use "medical help is on the way" as their key to entry.

In another section of the article with the sub-heading, "Change Through Struggle," the author leads us into the present-day situation quite effectively:

> The criminal role of the United States government and the mega
> corporations that it works for have been witnessed by the entire
> world over recent weeks encompassing the evolving epidemic. The
> greatly touted U.S. health care for-profit system has shown itself to
> be completely unable to handle the situation. (Wood, 2014).

The reason for that is because the goal is not to "handle the situation" as it relates to the Ebola crisis. The goal is to "take over the situation" and while they are going through the motions of working on some type of remedy they are hunkering down and establishing bases of contact around and within a particular country so that their fellow whites from America, Europe and other places can come to Africa and share in the spoils.

Moving on:

> On the other hand, socialist Cuba has won the hearts and minds of
> people across the world for the self-sacrifice and solidarity shown
> by its medical personnel, and its superior medical pathways of
> excellence in providing care and treatment to those who are sick
> and at risk of being sick. Even the imperialist media in the United
> States—The NY Times and the Wall Street Journal—have been
> forced to recognize and openly praise Cuba's outstanding
> intervention in West Africa. (Wood, 2014).

The reason why Cuba is respected in Africa is because Castro didn't just "talk the talk;" he "walked the walk." When black people were opposing the apartheid regime in South Africa, Castro sent some of his military there to help the African people engage in battle. This took place while the United States sat back and continued investing in South Africa. When it comes to Africa, America is consistently on the wrong side of history.

Wood's article continues:

> People in West Africa are struggling to respond and to defend their
> communities, with large numbers stepping forward to get involved

> with "the process" of defeating the disease. In the United States, Spain and elsewhere, workers are organizing to demand that hospitals and government agencies do whatever is necessary, spend whatever is required in dollars, to protect workers and support public health (Wood, 2014).

The problem is that "the process" is a white controlled one and the people who believe in that process are being bamboozled. African people have been tricked time and time again, and seem to be a part of two camps: (1) the ignorant who buy into whatever the west is peddling and (2) the sellouts and others who want a piece of the pie and will do whatever it takes to take advantage of the capital that the west spreads about in exchange for the assistance of these race traitors.

And then there is the "do-gooder" approach (akin to what Gates is doing today):

> One of the largest nurses' unions in the U.S., the National Nurses United has mobilized thousands of nurses to rally and sign petitions demanding action by the government and for-profit health corporations to provide the needed resources to make sure the disease does not spread. The union is calling strikes at hospitals across the United States on November 12, as part of a national day of action, to demand that all necessary funds are provided to ensure that all workers, patients and their families are protected from exposure. (Wood, 2014).

The "missionary syndrome" is alive and well; it seems that white people cannot help themselves. When they talk about giving assistance or offering resources, that is the first phase of their planned takeover of the area that they are seeking to invade and the people that they plan to pimp. Read a history book. In fact, Karenga (1967) once wrote that, "The white man has three ways of controlling blacks; the missionary, the mercenary and the military." And can there be any doubt that these "nurses groups" and others like Peace Corps and the rest have played a role in "softening up" the Motherland for eventual invasion by Caucasians?

And what is the situation today in 2017? According to the show "Fareed Zakaria GPS," aired April 9, 2017 there are 108 million people who face starvation in the world, most of them in Africa. In four African countries – S. Sudan, Nigeria, Somalia and Yemen – there are dire man-made humanitarian crises, mainly starvation. At present 1% of the Federal budget spent on foreign aid. So where is

Gates? Where is Buffett? Where are these rich white men who act as if they don't know what to do or who to give their money to?

"As Things Change," So They Remain the Same: Apartheid Then and Now

South Africa does not qualify as a kleptocracy because the masses of African people are so poor that there is nothing for the white minority to steal! White folks in South Africa controlled everything under the apartheid system, from education to energy, from the military and the media to mass transit. The lie is that apartheid changed once Nelson Mandela was "freed" but in my view that was all a façade. Whites still have the power and black people remain a "trying to catch up" majority.

An August 1, 2017 article from the Quora.com website titled, "Does Apartheid Still Exist in South Africa Today in Some Form?" offers some interesting insights on the current state of South Africa. The article, written by Onne Vegter, begins, as follows:

> The legal system of apartheid (which means separation or "apart-ness") no longer exists in South Africa today. It was abolished in 1994. However, although the laws have changed, the social and economic consequences of apartheid still exist today. (Vegter, 2017)

Well if the "social and economic consequences of apartheid" still exist today, then it was not "abolished." Like Jim Crow in America, the de jure aspects of the system were placed on hold and made to appear as if they were abolished, but the de facto reality of the system remains in full effect. The same can more likely than not be said about apartheid in South Africa.

The article continues:

> **The majority of white people still enjoy more privileges, better education, higher salaries, and are able to live in wealthier suburbs.** This dates back to apartheid, when the apartheid laws favoured white people and disadvantaged black people. (Vegter, 2017 – emphasis added)

If what was just described (in boldface) is the case, then apartheid did not end – it was merely modified. As long as the white man is in control and the racial gap remains wide, that is good enough for him and his white supremacist way of thinking. But black people are desperate for inclusion in a system that is really theirs by right and respond even more wimpishly than the "negroes" did in America when desegregation was "announced." Check it out:

> **Today, most people of colour in South Africa still live in poverty, receive a poor quality education which gives them few opportunities, and remain economically marginalized**. Most white people can afford to go to private hospitals, while most black people have to use the dysfunctional state hospitals. The unemployment percentage among black people is still much higher than among white people. **The townships, slums and informal settlements in South Africa are overwhelmingly black, while the wealthy, leafy neighbourhoods are mostly inhabited by whites. There is a fast-growing black middle class, however.** (Vegter, 2017 – emphasis added)

After describing the nature of apartheid while claiming it is no longer in existence, the author has the gall to claim that there "is a fast growing black middle class." That has to be bullshit. How can there be a fast-growing middle class in a segregated context? Where do they live? Where do they work? How are they educated? How did they reach that "Middle class" status? In America we have a term, "ghetto fabulous," which we use to describe black people who live above their means in terms of conspicuous consumption – big cars, fancy clothes and perhaps a nicer house than the others on the block – but they are still poor when it comes to actual wealth. This sounds like what is being described above.

> Having said all that, opportunities for skilled, professional black citizens are the same, if not more abundant than for white citizens of the same level of skill and education. **Competent black citizens who have managed to escape the townships and received a good education, are in high demand in many professions.** Most large companies are trying to meet **transformation targets** and score enough **BEE points (Black Economic Empowerment) to achieve their required BEE status**. Competent, skilled, black workers who communicate well, are honest and reliable team players, and have relevant tertiary qualifications and leadership skills, are in high demand and are extensively head-hunted in many different industries. So things are changing slowly. (Vegter, 2017)

Most racially segregated systems allow for tokenism and offer bullshit programs to avoid being charged with said segregation. In fact, take note of that so-called "Black Economic Empowerment" concept and the fact that you can get points. Guess what Warren Buffett's daughter has named a program for African-Americans in Omaha (after she stole the original "self-empowerment" concept from me)? She calls it the African-American Empowerment Network.

See how similarly racist minds think alike? By invoking the world "empowerment," black people can be duped into thinking that, like the Jeffersons of TV fame, they are "movin' on up"! The existence of "transformation targets" sounds a lot like a quota system from the days of American affirmative action. If the white man is at the top or in charge of it, those "targets" are going to be limited and very selective.

The half-assed article on apartheid (mercifully) concludes:

> **Racism still exists but it is frowned upon in South Africa**, and in recent times a number of people have been successfully prosecuted for posting racist comments or hate speech on social media. There is hope for South Africa. (Vegter, 2017)

White people are a minority and they are still calling the shots in the same way that they did under the apartheid system. Just because the white man says it doesn't make it so. There is hope for South Africa only if white people evacuate it or the population of black Africans increases by about 70%. In other words, there is no reason to "hope" for change because to go with that hope you need a plan. And hope, minus a plan, ain't nothin' but a dream.

Bill Gates and the Mandela Lecture: Critique and Commentary

Under the sub-heading, "The Youngest Continent," it is apparent that these white people have done their homework – or should I say "recon." After all, recon is short for "reconnaissance," and as those associated with the military will tell you, reconnaissance is, "military observation of a region to locate an enemy or ascertain strategic features" or in more everyday terms, "preliminary surveying or research."

White folks have always had their eyes on Africa. Back in the day they came forth with their bullshit religions and used that as a prelude for invasion. They came in and ripped off diamonds, gold, silver, bauxite and yes, even human bodies for enslavement. The same trends continue to day as these white people lust after oil and other natural resources. As someone always looking for an investment, why shouldn't Bill Gates join in to get his "piece of the rock"?

The lecture took place on July 17, 2016 and it follows. Gates is very long-winded but nevertheless, my views and analyses will filter in and out during his speech. Gates starts off, like so:

> I was 9 years old when Nelson Mandela was sent to prison on Robben Island. As a boy, I learned about him in school, and I

remember seeing reports about the anti-Apartheid movement on
the evening news. Decades later, I got to meet him and work with
him. In person he was even more inspiring than I had imagined.
His humility and courage left an impression that I will never
forget.

Here's my question: if you knew so much about the anti-apartheid movement, why didn't you do something about it? You were born with a silver spoon in your mouth: why didn't you support the anti-apartheid movement that was growing even as you were as a child? What did he do instead? He waited until he "grew up." Do you know how many people died while he waited and played in the yard with his horsey? Thousands.

South Africans, with their country asses, probably see this as some kind of compliment. After all, how else to explain the mentality of a group of black people who constitute 83% of the population, but who allow the white 17% to place them in ghettos called "Bantustans" and control them? We were less than 10% of the population here in a country far more powerful than South Africa and we managed to kick the white man's ass!

Gates continues:

So it was a special honor to be invited to give the Nelson Mandela
Lecture in Pretoria, South Africa. I eagerly accepted the invitation
and quickly began working on my remarks. I decided to share my
optimism about Africa's future—to explain why I think the
continent has the potential to change faster in the next generation
than any continent ever has.

Nice introduction, but here's my question: if this rich asshole hadn't been invited, what would he have done with his "beliefs" and theories regarding African's prospects and potential? You know what he would have done? He wouldn't have done a damn thing because the only reason Africa came to mind was because of that invitation. He's talking this shit because he's a smart guy and realizes that he can tap into the latent and untapped talent of the African people. He's doing to them what his white ancestors did to the continent: rape it for labor, natural resources and if he can find a way, for oil reserves!

At any rate, his speech begins:

It's because Africa is the world's youngest continent, and youth
can go hand in hand with a special dynamism. I was 20 years old
when Paul Allen and I started Microsoft. The entrepreneurs driving
startup booms in Johannesburg, Lagos, and Nairobi are just as
young, and the thousands of businesses they're creating are already

> changing lives across the continent. The potential will only grow as the digital revolution brings more advances in artificial intelligence and robotics.

When he and Paul Allen started Microsoft, Africa was the farthest thing from their racist, elitist minds. These young peckerwoods were nerds who were concerned about and committed to one thing: making money and making computers. Gates is only speaking in Africa now, long after the fact, because he can see a future market in the continent. The more young people, the more he can peddle his wares.

Gates continues:

> But positive change across Africa won't happen automatically. The real returns will come only if Africans can unleash this talent for innovation in all of the continent's growing population. That depends on whether all of its young people are given the opportunity to thrive.

This is paternalistic speaking and thinking. Nobody expects "change" to happen automatically and when it comes to the recipients of change being black people, we know better than that. Even the Christians know the value of "patience being a virtue," which of course I wholeheartedly disagree with. Be that as it may, the white man always stalls and buys time, anticipating an occasional fuckup along the way. But that's just the introduction to the new colonial thinking.

Take note where Gates is quick to add that, "The real returns will come only if Africans can unleash this talent for innovation in all of the continent's growing population." This means that he knows what the talent hasn't been "unleashed" thus far: because of white interference and intervention, that's why! They kidnapped millions of Africans from the continent, and those weren't winos, junkies and prostitutes being forced aboard those slave ships: some of those people were doctors and scientists and teachers. White people didn't give a shit, which is why once over in America these same white folks came up with the saying that, "an educated black man was a good field hand, spoiled."

Then, after placing the onus squarely on the shoulders of the descendants of the people that his (Gates') ancestors kidnapped and dehumanized, he throws in a little more white paternalism with the statement that the talent for innovation in the African population, " … depends on whether all of its young people are given the opportunity to thrive." The key words are "given" and "opportunity." Both of these words imply "help" from some source other than the Africans themselves, does it not? Who will be doing the giving? White interventionists like Gates. And who will define and then direct the Africans toward any "opportunities"? White men like Gates.

Like his pal Warren Buffett does in Omaha with the Sherwood Foundation, the Buffett Foundation and as Warren's sister does in Boston with the Lady Sunshine Foundation, these white people have to issue a global ego trip before they dole out the money. Therefore their act is not one of sincere benevolence; it is a public relations ruse. Gates closes out the introductory section of his videotaped speech as follows:

> It is still an open question, and it is the crux of my speech, which I gave today at the University of Pretoria. It was an honor to give this lecture, and I'm grateful to the Nelson Mandela Foundation and the university for inviting me. You can read my full speech below the video.
> Remarks as delivered
> Nelson Mandela Annual Lecture
> University of Pretoria, South Africa
> July 17, 2016

They "invited" him. Again, no act of voluntary benevolence. They invited him and he came. In other words, they leeched. So let's get that straight because you can't talk about post-colonial mindsets having changed without having eliminated the two fold economy of the colonized: begging for what they want and borrowing what they need. Africa remains as colonized after European exit in the same way that black people in America remain enslaved despite the so-called rule of the Emancipation Proclamation.

Now, the Gates speech begins:

> BILL GATES:
> Well, thank you. Good evening, ladies and gentlemen. Graça Machel, Professor Ndebele, Vice Chancellor de la Rey, members of the Mamelodi families, friends and dignitaries. I can't think of a greater honor than giving a lecture named after Nelson Mandela. I'm also thrilled that the theme of this lecture this year is "living together." It's truly fitting because in many ways, "living together" was also the theme of Nelson Mandela's life.

What did Gates know about Mandela other than the very things that the world had grown to know? What did he know about apartheid? What did he know about the Bureau of State Security (BOSS) and the identification passes that black people had to carry whenever they left the Bantustan? I believe he was just like any other white person: sit on the plane, study and cram some quick information, then make some references during the speech to make it appear as if you are some kind of expert or "kindred spirit" with the people you are speaking to.

As evidence, check out the following:

> The system he fought against was based on the opposite idea -- that people should be kept apart, that our superficial differences are more important than our common humanity. Today, South Africans are still striving to "live together" in the fullest sense. But you are so much closer to that ideal because Nelson Mandela and so many others believed in the promise of one South Africa.

How is the "system" that Mandela fought against any different than the one that Gates grew up in? America had its own form of apartheid – it was called "Jim Crow", remember? And even when outlawed in 1954, the belief in separation of the races continues on informally (de facto) to this very day in 2016. Gates is no different than any other out of touch white person who dares to traverse into the area of "race relations."

Check out where he claims, "South Africans are still striving to "live together" in the fullest sense. But you are so much closer to that ideal because Nelson Mandela and so many others believed in the promise of one South Africa." The fact is, black and white south Africans "lived together" under the apartheid regime, just as the corralled cattle and horses live on the same ranch as the farmer. Just as the "slaves in the shacks out back" lived on the same plantation as "the master" in the big house. Living together is not the issue because white people can tolerate that much: it's living together and keeping them out of our damn business and off our backs that has been the perennial problem!

I don't care who the figureheads in South Africa are – the white man still remains firmly in control. He is in control of the banking system, the financial district, the hotel district, the tourism industry and all other institutions that truly count, including the educational system South African blacks are among the most docile and anglo-loving once they get over to the American states for study. They appear to love people. They had a young brutha named Mark Mathane and once he married a white woman he thought he was in seventh heaven. He wrote a book and went on tour with it. The title was *Kaffir Boy*, which translates to mean Nigger Boy. And he was proud of it!

Pretending as if he has kept up with Mandela's life, Gates claims, "I was only nine years old when Nelson Mandela was sent to Robben Island. As a boy, I learned about him in school. I remembered seeing reports about the anti-Apartheid movements regularly on the evening news." The evening news. Here's my question: what did he do about what he learned from those news reports once he got to school? Did he share the information with his "chums"? Did he organize an anti-apartheid effort to show solidarity with South African people? Did he speak on campus about what he had learned? Did he write an essay for the local newspaper?

The answer to all of these queries is "no." Gates didn't do shit. And yet take note of what he claims next:

> The first time I got to speak to him was in 1994 when he called me to help fund South Africa's election. I was running Microsoft, and largely focused on software most of the time, but I admired him so much, and I knew the election was historic. So I did what I could to help. My first trip to Africa had been just the year before that in 1993 when my wife Melinda and I had traveled to East Africa.

So even after he grew up, it was Gates who had to be contacted to speak. He volunteered or donated nothing. He was running Microsoft and claims that he did what he could to help. Did he? Is there any doubt he could have done more? By his own admission the first time he visited South Africa was after he had traveled to East Africa. By the way, *where* in East Africa? While "South Africa" is a proper noun, East Africa is not. This is as foolish a statement as the white people make when they tell you they "went to Africa," as if Africa is a small town somewhere. They don't respect "the Dark Continent" (a name white folks gave to it) enough to deal with the nations and countries individually. Gates apparently is no different.

Even in describing visits to Africa, white people continue to talk about an entire continent as if it were a hamlet or a township. For example, observe the following:

> The landscape was beautiful, the people were friendly, but the poverty there, which we were seeing for the first time, disturbed us. It also energized us. Obviously, we knew parts of Africa were poor, but being on the continent turned what had been an abstraction into an injustice we couldn't ignore.

The landscape and the people. Of which sector? Of what area? Which tribe? You see? This is that old "seen-one-nigga-you-seen-'em-all" mentality that white people seem to share. For instance if you tell them that you visited California many will ask, "Do you know John? He's from California," implying that all black people know each other. You hear it all the time. And what you just read in Gates' own words shows that when all is said and done, he is no different.

The next issue I would like to address is where he states, "we knew parts of Africa were poor, but being on the continent turned what had been an abstraction into an injustice we couldn't ignore." He is the one who is dealing in abstractions with his own descriptions! And if he knew about the poverty, why didn't he do something as soon as he learned about it? The time he spent giving computers to colleges and nonprofits in wealthy America could have been spent putting some running water into some of those villages or setting up electrical plants! Like Warren Buffett, these kind of people are blind to obvious manifestations of poverty, opting to donate and contribute to "causes" where they, in turn, can come off like missionaries.

Gates continues:

> Melinda and I had always known that we'd give our wealth to philanthropy eventually. But when we were confronted with such glaring inequity, we started thinking about how to take action sooner. This sense of urgency was further spurred on by another trip in 1997 when I came to Johannesburg for the first time as a representative of Microsoft.

How long did it take these rich white people to "decide" when it would be an opportune time to say "enough is enough" as it relates to the "glaring inequity" that they claim they saw? After all, such inequity had been in existence since before they were born and being the scholars that they are, surely they read about it in high school and college. But they took their time and during that time, tens of thousands of people all over the African continent died from starvation, dysentery, thirst, diabetes and a host of preventable ailments. But as usual when it comes to black people, the white philosophy seems to be, "better late than never."

Even when he claims to care about poverty the best Gates seems to be able to do is peripheral. Check out the following:

> I spent most of the time in the richer part of the city in business meetings, but I also went to the community center in Soweto where Microsoft was donating computers.

So despite all his awareness of the problems, despite all of his "commitment" to doing something about those problems, Gates not only took his time but when he arrived on the continent he went to places where he felt most comfortable. After all, South Africa does have some of the most expensive and lavish hotels in the world. So he shells out his American Express card so he and Melinda could have a nice, comfortable suite, and then after a nice night's rest and a great dinner and room service, decides to visit an impoverished area, Soweto. Oh, and by the way, Soweto is the home of the June 1976 Soweto riots. In a nutshell,

> Students from numerous Sowetan schools began to protest in the streets of Soweto in response to the introduction of Afrikaans as the medium of instruction in local schools ... It is estimated that 20,000 students took part in the protests. They were met with fierce police brutality. The number of protesters killed by police is usually given as 176, but estimates of up to 700 have been made ... In remembrance of these events, the 16th of June is now a public holiday in South Africa, named Youth Day (Wikipedia, 2016).

Black kids died, and Gates read about it. He turned on the television and if he was paying attention , he heard about it. Did he move right away to put his millions and his computers into action? Of course not. He waited until the time was right for *him*. He finally went to Soweto and tells the crowd he is speaking to, "My visit to Soweto, which was quite different then than it is now, taught me how much I had to learn about the world outside the comfortable bubble I'd lived in all my life." He can make all the excuses he wants, but we know the truth: when you have money you can fly anywhere in the world any time you want to. It comes down to the issue of priorities: what is important and what is not. Africa was not important to him because he's white. When he got some leisure time, that is only when he decided to take Africa into consideration.

Now he shifts into "Jesus the savior mode":

> As I walked into the community center, I noticed there weren't any electrical connections. To keep the computer on, the one I was donating, they had rigged up an extension cord connected to a diesel generator outside. I realized the minute I left, the generator would get moved to something more important.

How did he "realize" what would happen "the minute" he left? And if he saw this taking place and is so in tune with the future, then why not bring some generators along with him, or some spare extension cords? He came in for a "tour" of a place that he knew was lacking in even the most basic of amenities. And yet he brought *nothing*. He continues with his pontificating:

> So as I read my remarks about the importance of the technology gap, I knew that it was only a small part of the story. Computers could help people do very important things, and in fact, they are part of how life on the continent can be revolutionized. But computers alone can't feed disease or cure children. And if they can't be turned on, they can't do much at all. So after that, Melinda and I moved to start our foundation because the cost of waiting had become clear.

The cost was always "clear," he just took his damn time to fit dealing with the cost into his "busy schedule." After all, black people are secondary human beings when it comes to rich white people. They have their golf club memberships, beauty appointments and stocks to check into. Then, when they look around for something to do, they look at black people the same way a person would look at a dog in a cage at the humane society. They want to "adopt" and "help" us, but they don't want to address the material and subjective conditions that impact on black lives.

So far all Gates has done is mouth liberal platitudes and general truisms. But his lecture continues:

> Our work is based on the simple idea that every person, no matter where they live, should have the opportunity to lead a healthy and productive life. We've spent the past 15 years learning about the issues and looking for the leverage points where we can do the most to help people seize their opportunity.

Why would it take fifteen years to learn something that was "a simple idea"? Do you see what I'm getting at? When it comes to black people, these rich white people take their sweet time until the conditions become so bad that once they decide to act, anything that they do will be considered an act of benevolence! Just like cops who sit on a drug house for months supposedly to "build a case." Why wait so long? Because they want to make sure the drug money is going to be at the same location so they can bust in, arrest the dealers, take some of the money and turn in a small portion of it. Not only that, but the longer they wait, the more black lives get destroyed by the dealers whose customers are the low-income people that the cops claim to be out to protect.

So Gates admits that he and Melinda took their sweet time addressing the issue. Then he turns around and makes the following claim:

> It was when I started coming to Africa regularly for the foundation that I got to know Nelson Mandela personally. AIDS was one of the first issues our foundation worked on, and Nelson Mandela was both an advisor and an inspiration.

If Mandela was such an inspiration, why did it take so long to get things started? If Gates was coming to Africa "regularly" (remember that Africa is the continent, not the South African nation), why did it take "foundation business" to get this ultra-rich white man to act on what he had observed? If Mandela was such an "advisor and inspiration," why didn't he simply take out a large loan from his "pal" Gates and get to work right away? All of this smacks of bullshit and makes

Gates sound like some kind of savior just because he delivered on some donations a day late and a dollar short. In the meantime, how many African bruthas and sistahs died?

And it's partially Mandela's fault as well. I never had much respect for a man who could serve 27 years in a South African prison and then, once released, divorce his wife because he learned she had an affair with another man while he was locked up. What?? Winnie needed some dick, too! She is a human being who stood by him all that time. Just because she got a nut or two while he was in prison didn't mean she loved him any less. In fact, she took over the "movement" and held it together while he was in the joint!

At any rate, pay close attention to the following:

> One thing we talked about was the stigma around AIDS. So I remember 2005 very clearly when his own son died of AIDS. Rather than stay silent about the cause of his son's death, Nelson Mandela announced it publicly because he knew that stopping the disease required breaking down the walls of fear and shame that surrounded it.

"Talked"? The time for talking was over with. That's the problem now: people want to "talk" about the problems in and around Africa, but very few people want to take any concrete action! The "stigma around AIDS"? Fuck the stigma: talk about the damn cure! His son probably died of AIDS because he was on drugs or was taking it up the ass. The reason Mandela stayed silent was probably because he found out that his son was gay! Maybe that was the basis for his anger being directed toward Winnie, who knows?

Then comes the ridiculous conclusion that Mandela "knew that stopping the disease required breaking down the walls of fear and shame that surrounded it." No, that was ONE of the concerns, not the main one. The main concern was working on a cure and promoting it and the success rate for a cure would then end the stigma! The stigma was that AIDS was a "gay disease" and that meant that the disdain was directed toward the homosexual community as well as the disease. So first of all, stop assuming that only gay people get the disease and then start working on some approaches toward addressing the AIDS epidemic. Hey Gates: build a fuckin' hospital!

Continuing:

> It is important to recall Nelson Mandela's legacy, and I'm grateful for the opportunity to do so. But Nelson Mandela was concerned about the future. He believed people could make the future better

than the past. And so that's what I want to focus on for the
remainder of my talk.

Making the future better than the past should be a piece of cake when you're talking about black people in South Africa. They had been repressed, brutalized and holed up in "Bantustans" for a century and therefore things couldn't really get any worse. The future is what Gates claims that he's going to focus on. But as you will see, many of his comments smack of the same kind of white hypocrisy that always seems to raise its head whenever the topic has anything to do with the African continent.

If Mandela was so concerned about the future, why didn't he chase DeKlerk and those other racist bastards out of South Africa as soon as he got free? He forgave those peckerwoods knowing full well that their laws and actions were responsible for the deaths of tens of thousands of black people. He had the nerve to take pictures actually posing with those South African white boys. The future? What – as a lobotomized robot for the post-apartheid regime?

Then Gates has the nerve to ask, "What can South Africa become? What can Africa become? What can the world become? And what must we do to make it that way?" In my view these are two different sets of paradigms. Asking what South Africa can become seems to connote self-reliance and doing what it takes, on its own, to rebuild itself. But then the paternalistic racist asks, "What must we do to make it that way?" then it becomes the same ol' missionary syndrome, the same ol' "white man to the rescue" motif that permeates their version of world history and in reality, usually paves the way for an eventual undermining and then take over of whatever country they've set their eyes on.

Gates already has a name for his "contribution." Check it out:

> The Millennium Development Goals adopted by the United
> Nations in 2000 laid a foundation that enabled the world, including
> Africa, to achieve extraordinary progress over the last 15 years.

The United Nations is nothing more than an adjunct to the United States. Those national leaders bring their robe-wearing asses to America for the meetings at the UN Building and spend more time getting drunk and chasing white bitches than they do anything else. Add to that this plan called "The Millennium Development" and its "goals," and what you have is a takeover. I don't see the achievement of any "extraordinary goals over the last 15 years." Whose goals were accomplished? Africa as a continent is still being dominated by outside forces and military dictators, and South Africa is heavily reliant on white tourism more than anything else. You call that a *plan*?

Continuing:

> And the Sustainable Development Goals that recently replaced them set even more ambitious targets for creating the better world we all want. When I talk about progress, I always start with child survival because whether children are living or dying is such a basic indicator of a society's values.

The white man is never going to change. Like Warren Buffett, Bill and Melinda Gates are willing to "invest," but they don't actually put money in the hands of the people that they claim to want to help. As is the case with Buffett, all of those benevolence is conditional. And the method of operation is similar to that of Susie Buffett and her emphasis on young minds: control the babies and you control the race. That has long been a tactic of oppressors the world over. And take note of what Gates says above: "I always start with child survival because whether children are living or dying is such a basic indicator of a society's values."

That's why the name of the "project" is "Sustainable Development." You "sustain" the development of a people by controlling that development. That is how the program or the goals are "sustained": you stay on site and give orders and dole out money as needed. Everything is in your name and you expand your asset base. This is not free money or free resources the way that the Gates' attempt to make it look. They are Johnny-come-latelys who found a niche that they could exploit and the name of that niche is South Africa.

> Since 1990, child mortality in sub-Saharan Africa has been reduced by 54 percent. That means one million fewer children dying each year compared to 25 years ago. Ten African countries achieved the very ambitious MDG target of reducing child mortality by over two-thirds.

Since 1990 child mortality has been reduced. So what? Where was Gates sitting when he was reading that data from 1990, about 26 years before he was giving this speech? If whoever did the study can exhibit these kinds of statistics, then what are they doing in other spheres of human activity? You want to brag about infant mortality being reduced but you don't do anything about the murders of African teenagers and children on the other end of the spectrum, which makes it a zero sum game. Tell the whole truth, white man!

Continuing:

> At the same time, the incidence of poverty and malnutrition is down. And though economic growth has slowed in the past few

> years, it's been very robust in many African countries for more
> than a decade. This is real progress, but the Africa Rising narrative
> doesn't tell the whole story about the life on the continent.

See my point? They want to talk about fewer babies dying but on the other end those babies are going to experience malnutrition and mal-nourishment. In simpler terms, the babies are being born so that they can die almost right away!

The Africa Rising narrative cannot be positive as long as the white man is making the rules. The black people in charge aren't much better. I know South Africans, having been married to one for over 35 years. When you consider the oppression that they faced, the murderous brutality of the apartheid government over there, you would be shocked to see how quickly they come over here to America and start kissing white ass almost immediately. I saw it take place at the University of Iowa and in my own household as "white friend" after "white friend" was invited over to my black nationalist digs by my beautiful South African wife who had the nerve to be a part of the anti-Apartheid movement.

So don't tell me about South Africa. I've studied it and written on it. I know that when 83% of the population is too gutless to pick up a brick, march to Pretoria and knock those peckerwoods in the head, something is wrong. We did it here in America and we were less than ten percent of the population! That stuff that Gates is spewing are the words of a neo-colonialist: he uses the people who look like the ones he wants to control in order to make money, make investments and do it all under the guise of "philanthropy."

Gates adds that,

> First, the progress have been uneven. You know this very well here
> in South Africa. In last year's Nelson Mandela Annual Lecture, the
> French economist, Thomas Piketty, pointed out that income
> inequality in South Africa is, quote, "--higher than pretty much
> anywhere else in the world."

Gates is a day late and literally a dollar short, as usual. This peckerwood quotes another white man about the situation in South Africa. Thomas Piketty, according to my sources, is "a French economist who works on wealth and income inequality. He is a professor at the École des hautes études en sciences sociales, associate chair at the Paris School of Economics and Centennial professor at the London School of Economics new International Inequalities Institute."

A Frenchman invited in to tell Africans what to do. As a Black Studies instructor I recall well that by 1900 much of Africa had been colonized by seven European powers—Britain, France, Germany, Belgium, Spain, Portugal, and Italy.

After the conquest of African decentralized and centralized states, the European powers set about establishing colonial state systems. France was right there. And now here is one of their scholars once again, digging in and getting paid. This is the "Tarzan syndrome" combined with the "Robinson Crusoe syndrome" all over again!

Where are the black African scholars? Where are the scholars from countries of color. Those South African assholes make me sick: after all that shit that Pic Botha and DeKlerk put those black bastards through and it seems that they just can't get over kissing the white man's ass! They have a lecture series named after Mandela – whose commitment I question – and then they invite crackers in to tell them what to do. What is that shit about?

The income inequality exists because of white people. The Boers who came in and stole the diamonds. The white corporations that are settling in and ripping of other resources while those black South Africans live like kings in high rise hotels and kiss as much white ass as they can have access to. The result is that black people make more than they did before, but they don't make nearly as much as the white man. The same can be said of blacks in America: we make more now than we did during slavery (when we made nothing), but the income inequality is as high here as it is in South Africa. Damn what Gates has to say about it.

Then come more half-truths which, of course, are tantamount to lies:

> In general, African countries tend to have higher rates of inequality than countries on other continents. And despite healthy average GDP growth in the region, many countries have not yet shared in it. Inequalities exist within countries and between countries. So until progress belongs to all people everywhere, the real promise of living together will remain elusive.

Check out this revisionist and his claim that, "In general, African countries tend to have higher rates of inequality than countries on other continents." Why is that? Because Africa is the only BLACK continent, that's why! And it's also a continent that white colonial powers have raped time and time again. White incursion is what led to the divestment of Africa's natural resources, the abduction of hundreds of thousands of Africans for enslavement, and overall colonial control. Why didn't the liberal Gates offer these explanations regarding the ORIGINS of the inequality rather than merely stating the obvious?

Then he somersaults over talking about the sources of the inequality and the racism and colonialism that created it to a discussion of grandiose and idealistic schemes. He says, "So until progress belongs to all people everywhere, the real promise of living together will remain elusive." How can progress belong to "all people"? What would it be based on? Who would make the decisions about or pull the switches that would enable this "progress" to become a reality? Gates doesn't know and he was lying when he said it. Evidence can be found in his own words:

> Second, even with the great progress Africa has made, it still lags behind the rest of the world in most indicators. In sub-Saharan Africa, one in 12 children still die before they turn five. Now, that's a vast improvement compared to 25 years ago, but African children are still 12 times more likely to die than the average child in the world.

Great progress? By whose standards? If you take four steps backward and then take four steps forward, you haven't made progress – you're back where you started! And in all truth, Africa's not even at THAT point? African leaders are destroying their countries, hording money and resources and using military power to keep the masses down – a veritable kleptocracy in some cases. Gates is a smart man – he can see this. So when he avoids an issue, it is on purpose. He has a point to make and he can't make it if he exposes the REAL devils behind the demise of Africa – members of HIS race!

Sounding much like Thomas Malthus and Paul Ehrlich before him, Gates starts dropping "population bomb-type" messages on the African throng:

> And because rates of poverty and malnutrition aren't shrinking as fast as the population is growing, the number of people who are poor or malnourished has actually gone up since 1990.
> Finally, the progress is fragile. The continent's two largest economies, here in South Africa and in Nigeria, are facing serious economic challenges. And new threats require attention. The Ebola crisis pointed out weaknesses in many national health systems. The effects of climate change are already being felt among farmers in many countries.

Take note that he knows which nations have the largest economies on the continent, and he names them. So why didn't he mention the fact that the reason that they are "facing serious economic challenges" is because of the incursion and intrusion of white nations, including the United States? South Africa, the United States and Israel were part of the "tri-lateral alliance" that got together to keep the apartheid system in South Africa going full bore. And Nigeria sold out to the United States a long time ago, exchanging its oil for "free education" in America. In other words, something worth something for something worth nothing but tendencies toward assimilation.

Therefore, according to Gates,

> In short, to meet the ambitious goals of the Sustainable Development Goals, Africa needs to do more, do it faster, and make sure everybody benefits. It won't be easy, but I believe it can be done.

Instructions from someone who could be doing more himself. He has the financial wherewithal to get a lot done. I'm talking infrastructure, job creation and development, enhanced educational opportunities and so on. But note that he has shifted the context from South Africa to the continent in general. That's like talking about America and then shifting the discussion to the problems of the North American continent.

You see, the problem with Gates, Warren Buffett and people like them are that they know what needs to be done but won't do it. They want to make grand gestures about giving away their money, but then they give it away to their fellow race-members who are, in varying degrees, all part of the problem. They want to get the photo opportunity and the international publicity associated with a so-called "concern" for the African continent, but they don't want to put I stopgap measures to neutralize the imperialism and colonialism that still continue to take place and hamper African progress.

Gates was out making money and expanding his computer empire while the African continent was being pillaged by European and American interests. Now that he has finally found the time, check out what he has the gall to tell the audience:

> The successes and failures of the past 15 years have generated examples and lessons we can follow. Phenomenal advances in science and technology are expanding the range of solutions available to solve development challenges. And then there is the ingenuity of the African people.

The last sentence is the only one that applies to Africa. The other statements about the "examples and lessons", the "phenomenal advances" and the "expansion of the range of solutions" are all about white interests and those external to the continent. The last line, which points to the "ingenuity of the African people" is nothing new: the white man saw that upon his initial encounters with the African people. He then proceeded to steal everything he could, pilfer every idea and that activity continued upon the kidnaps and enslavement of African people once they were brought to American shores.

Next come the references to Mandela's statements – implying that he (Gates) and Mandela were best pals:

> One topic that Nelson Mandela came back to over and over again
> was the power of youth. He knew what he was talking about
> because he started his career as a member of the African National
> Congress Youth League when he was still in his 20s.
> Later on, he understood that highlighting the oppression of young
> people was a powerful way to explain why things must change.
> There is a universal appeal to the conviction that youth deserve a
> chance.

Africa has always been about the youth. What Mandela was talking about was therefore an extension of what he had been taught. The African nationalist flag colors of red, black and green clearly show that red is for the blood, black is for the color of our skin, and green is for the youth. The youth are the future. As a member of the African National Congress this information was known throughout the land. Gates claims to have known all this about Mandela and yet he didn't act on what he knew until he took care of his capitalist business first. That "universal appeal" that youth deserve a chance has been ringing from the mountain tops of Africa and Black America for centuries. When did Gates finally get a clue and decide to do something about it?

Gates adds,

> I agree with Mandela about young people, and that is one reason I
> am optimistic about the future of this continent. Demographically,
> Africa is the world's youngest continent. And its youth can be the
> source of a special dynamism.

If the white man knows about Africa's youth, then what do you think he is planning? He is thinking about ways to co-opt and control that youth, the way he does with every "colored" nation he comes into contact with. The same way he did the Native American kids when he forced them into boarding schools so that they could reject their own culture and, in doing so, reject themselves. This is the white man's modus operandi: control the youth of a people and you control the future of those people. Old people are set in their ways and are less likely to be ordered around and more likely to put their foot in your ass. But if you can tease and tantalize youth, pacify and placate them, then you can win them over and, if need be, use their energy and effort and turn it against their own people.

Now comes the statistic that could spell doom for black people if we don't hurry up and take control. According to Gates,

> In the next 35 years, two billion babies will be born in Africa. By 2050, 40 percent of the entire world's children will live on this continent.

Two billion African babies in the next 35 years? Now can you see why all of a sudden white boys like Gates have an interest in the continent. No, not as a support system but as exploiters. That many people have to be controlled, and the white man is an expert and neo=colonial control. This form of control means taking the people who look like you and using them to direct and dominate the fate and future of those children. Forty percent of the entire world's children on the African continent? Add that to the billions of Chinese and the white man doesn't have much of a chance, now does he. The white race has seen this coming for a long time, as Dr. Frances Cress Welsing originally pointed out in Black Scholar magazine in May of 1974 and later reiterated in her book *The Isis Papers*:

> The Color-Confrontation theory further postulates that whites are vulnerable to their sense of numerical inadequacy. This inadequacy is apparent in their drive to divide the vast majority of non-whites into fractional, as well as frictional, minorities. This is viewed as a fundamental behavioral response of whites to their own minority status. The white "race" has structured and manipulated their own thought processes and conceptual patterns, as well as those of the entire non-white world majority, so that the real numerical minority (whites) illusionally feels and represents itself as the world's majority, while the true numerical majority (non-whites) illusionally feels and views itself as the minority (Welsing, 1991, p. 10).

This fact is all the more reason why white domination, through its technological advances, is so important. Black people have the numbers and the reproductive ability, but the latter can be controlled through technology and social control. Numbers: this means the white man is going to have to change the game. This means that there must be more black people who do the white man's bidding by thinking just like them. Witness the rise of Ben Carson, a submissive neurosurgeon who is now Director of Housing and Urban Development. Witness the likes of Omarosa Manigault, Paris Dennard, Michael Steele and other Uncle Toms who are given incredible amounts of TV time to essentially provide a rubber stamp to whatever the white man says.

The Gates pontifications continue:

> Economists talk about a demographic dividend. When you have more people of working age and fewer dependents for them to take

> care of, you can generate phenomenal economic growth. Rapid
> economic growth in East Asia in the 1970s and 1980s was partly
> driven by the large number of young people moving into their
> workforce.

That was Asia, which has an entirely different cultural and economic apparatus than Africa. Gates knows that. Plus he just mentioned the youth explosion that was going to be taking place then turns around and says that when you have fewer dependents for working class people then you can generate phenomenal economic growth. But young people ARE dependents! So what is this white man trying to say and do with this presentation? He avoids this question and quickly claims that, "But for me, the most important thing about young people is the way their minds work. Young people are better than old people at driving innovation because they're not locked in by the limits of the past." But they are still dependent until they reach adulthood!

Now comes the ego-driven ethnocentric part of the presentation where Gates, after showing how dependent Africa is going to be, promotes his own youth and independence:

> When I started Microsoft at the age of 19, computer science was a
> young field. We didn't feel beholden to old notions about what
> computers could or should do. We dreamed about the next big
> thing and we scoured the world around us for the ideas and tools
> that would help us create it. But it wasn't just Microsoft. Steve
> Jobs was 21 when he started Apple. Mark Zuckerberg was only 19
> when he started Facebook.

How can you compare white boys who have the benefit of white privilege, backing from banks and from well-to-do associates with what is taking place on Africa, a continent that these same white boys have pimped over the past several centuries? It's easy for Gates to ego trip and to give kudos to Steve Jobs and Zuckerberg now that they've built virtual empires. But while they were building and amassing their hundreds of millions, did they bother to think about Africa? Hell no. But now all of a sudden they are because of the reasons mentioned in this paper because Africa can be easily co-opted, the people can be duped into assimilating into white culture, and the youthful future can therefore be channeled into doing the bidding of these white computer nerds.

Evidence backing up this allegation follows:

> The African entrepreneurs driving startup booms in the Silicon
> Savannahs from Johannesburg and Cape Town to Lagos and

> Nairobi are just as young in chronological age, but also in their outlook. The thousands of businesses they're creating are already changing daily life across the continent.

African entrepreneurs? That's like saying "black businessmen in America." In both cases you have people who put on suits and ties, drive around in foreign cars and have a building. But their supplies, funding, merchandise and so on is usually provided by the white man. You can't have a black night club unless you by the liquor from the white man; you can't have a black computer store unless you buy the white man's knick-knacks; you can't have a black supermarket unless you buy food from white farmers and major food suppliers. So when these people talk about "African entrepreneurs," they are intentionally using misleading language. It's akin to what Dr. Carter G. Woodson talked about long ago in his book, *Mis-Education of the Negro* when he shared the following about "cooperation:"

> Cooperation implies equality of the participants in the particular task at hand. On the contrary, however, the usual way now is for the whites to work out their plans behind closed doors, have them approved by a few Negroes serving nominally on a board, and then employ a white or mixed staff to carry out their program. This is not interracial cooperation. It is merely the ancient idea of calling upon the "inferior" to carry out the orders of the "superior." To express it in post-classic language, as did Jessie O. Thomas, "The Negroes do the 'coing' and the whites the 'operating'" (Woodson, 1933: p. 29).

And this is how it seems to function. Even Ebony magazine doesn't own the paper that it prints that magazine on. Dr. Woodson was correct 84 years ago, and it stands correct today in world politics, in regional politics and in national politics. Look at the Congressional Black Caucus, the NAACP, the National Urban League and those other coons. They get to wear the white man's suits and ties, attend his banquets and they think that progress had been made. All this when the plight or black people has not markedly improved for centuries. And how could it when the relationship between the master and the enslaved remains the same? Gates is fully aware of this fact.

Gates' presentation continues:

> In a few days, I'll be meeting with some of these young innovators. People like the 21-year-old who founded Kenya's first software coding school to provide other young people with computer programming skills. And like the 23-year-old social

> entrepreneur here in South Africa who manufactures school bags
> from recycled plastic shopping bags. Besides being highly visible
> to protect children as they're walking to school, these school bags
> sport a small solar panel that charges a lantern during the journey
> to and from school, providing illumination so students can study at
> home.

Meeting with these young people is one thing, financing them is another. These white people like to, and are known for, stealing ideas from the Motherland and then re-branding those ideas here in the states and taking credit. This kind of co-optation and theft has a long history. If these kids are smart they will enlist the help of a trained attorney (one who won't be open to being bribed) and get some copyrights and trademarks on the books before trusting some white billionaire who knows nothing about African culture other than what he hastily read the night before this speech.

Gates makes promises that I do not believe he has the power or intention on keeping. Check it out:

> The full returns will come if we can multiply this talent for
> innovation by the whole of Africa's growing youth population.
> That depends on whether Africa's young people -- all of Africa's
> young people -- are given the opportunity to thrive.

Full returns? Does he mean for the continent or for the continent and a kickback for America? These peckerwoods have NEVER done anything for free. Even their Peace Corp and those international ministries go in with the Bible in one hand and a contract in the other stipulating some kind of return in human or capital resources. How can you "give all of Africa's young people the opportunity to thrive" when you have the relatives of Africans right here in America who are starving to death, being beaten down by cops in the streets, are dying from inadequate health care, being mis-educated from pre-school through college and suffering from sky-high infant mortality rates?

More of Gates' rhetoric continues in a vintage "missionary" manner:

> Nelson Mandela said, "Poverty is not natural, it is man made and it
> can be overcome and eradicated by the actions of human
> beings."We are the human beings that must take action. And we
> have to decide now because this unique moment won't last. We
> must clear away the obstacles that are standing in young people's
> way so that they can seize all of their potential …

Perhaps Gates is telling on himself. After his bloviating about poverty and human potential, what is his advice: that young people should "seize' their potential. Not go after it, not pursue it, not strive for it – but 'seize it'. In order to seize something, you have to forcibly take ahold of it. Why would kids with potential have to use force unless the source they were seizing it from was opposing them? In other words: white folks! And who would know better than Gates, who took his sweet time before heading to Africa to offer help?

And he adds,

> If young people are sick and malnourished, their bodies and brains will never fully develop. If they are not educated well, their minds will lie dormant. If they do not have access to economic opportunities, they will not be able to achieve their goals.

And remember: he knew this all along and in fact, had known it for decades. What took him so long to act on what he knew? Why now? Why in the name of "Nelson Mandela" in the country of South Africa when he's got thirty million African-Americans in the United States who need to be adopted? I'll tell you why: Africans have the land and they have the natural resources. They also have a Tarzan mentality when it comes to their views of white people: they seem to adore these crackers while at the same time looking down their noses at their brothers and sisters here in the United States. Gates knows this – and this is what he is counting on.

Moving on:

> But if we invest in the right things, if we make sure the basic needs of Africa's young people are taken care of, then they will have the physical, cognitive, and emotional resources they need to change the future. Life on this continent will improve faster than it ever has. And the inequities that have kept people apart will be erased by broad-based progress that is the very meaning of the words "living together."

Gates has it ass backwards. The people on the continent were "living together" before the white man came. The people on the continent had the physical, cognitive and emotional resources they needed before European intervention. Africa is where it is today because of the interruptions and incursions of the white race. This is a point that Gates is probably aware of but refuses to mention, relying on South African fear and ignorance of the past.

The Gates speech continues:

> When Melinda and I started our foundation 15 years ago, we asked ourselves: What are the areas of greatest impact? It was clear to us that investing in health was high on the list. When people aren't healthy, they can't turn their attention to other priorities. But when health improves, life improves by every measure.

The topic that was selected by Gates and his wife was not the point. The point was the geographic area where "health" would be emphasized and invested in. Clearly, if it took fifteen years from them to get their pale asses to South Africa, then the Motherland was not a priority. Their first priority was their white brothers and sisters who are bilking the American public in the name of "cancer research," "AIDS research" and those other scams that they keep talking about on the major media while Africa is hardly ever mentioned.

And yet according to Gates,

> Over the last 15 years, our foundation has invested more than $9 billion in Africa. And we are committed to keep on investing to help Africa. In the next five years, we will invest another $5 billion.

Investing in Africa is not the same thing as donating or giving. They may have purchased some land, a few buildings or some other asset that they will get a return on. But investing is one thing, donating is quite another. Nine billion dollars is a lot of money, so tell me: what came of it? What can they point to that shows progress and development? Furthermore, Africa is a continent, not a country. So why are they talking about continental investment to the South African people? That would be like me saying I invested nine billion in North America. Okay – so how much did the United States get?

Gates further claims that,

> Some of this money has gone into discovering and developing new and better vaccines and drugs to help prevent infectious disease. We've also invested in global partnerships that work closely with countries across the continent to get these solutions to the people who need them most. We've been fortunate to work with amazing partners, and together we've seen incredible progress.

Who is "we"? Is he talking about the World Health Organization? If he is, then he's not telling the whole story. White people brought their diseases with them from Europe and landed squarely on these shores, infecting and killing off huge numbers of Native Americans. When you only wash your ass once a week, when you don't even wipe it after taking a crap, and when your woman doesn't douche, then you can expect some serious diseases. And here they are now, hundreds of years later, having the GALL to spread the word about "cures" and "combating infections." As the song taught, "Don't believe the hype."

When a billionaire white man uses the term, "incredible progress," he is speaking financially or economically. And he is speaking personally. Why else would he care – he has all the money he needs! Those words are teasers laid out for gullible audiences. They know Gates is a billionaire so the tendency for those who are in the audience is to take what he says as if it is god's law. Just as Warren Buffett is dubbed "the oracle of Omaha," Gates is seen in the same way and he knows it. And both of these men – Buffett and Gates – know that people view them in this way and therefore they tend to be lax with certain facts and they can easily cover up their ignorance on racial issues.

Gates moves on:

> For example, the entire continent of Africa has been polio free for
> two years, which puts us within reach of wiping polio out from the
> face of the earth forever. The newest vaccines that protect children
> from two of the most devastating diseases -- pneumonia and
> diarrhea -- are reaching children across Africa at the same time
> they're available for children in wealthier countries.

The issue is not who is getting cured on the continent; it's *who brought it there in the first place?* Who divested the Motherland of natural resources, wealth and human capital to the point where it was left vulnerable and victim to the attacks of the invading colonial powers? Those people who were kidnapped for purposes of enslavement were not just some run-of-the-mill scum types, criminals or hobos. These types would describe the white people who were kicked out of England and then "banished" to America and Australia. No, the black people who were kidnapped were healers, doctors, engineers, craftsmen and so on. This gargantuan rape of the continent is what left it vulnerable to the types of diseases that Gates herein describes.

Furthermore,

> Countries that invest in strong, community-based primary
> healthcare systems -- including Malawi, Ethiopia, and Rwanda --
> are making great progress reducing child mortality.
> Malaria infections and deaths are down significantly thanks to
> better treatment and prevention tools.

This proves my point. The "investment" in the primary healthcare systems that Gates is describing could have been made much sooner had it not been for the intrusion of colonial powers along with the outside interference from the United States and Russia. Gates is a Johnny-come-lately and is talking as if he had been there all along. The fact is, Gates didn't even act on what he knew many decades ago as it relates to Africa's on-going health problems; he just stood back, watched and bided his time.

More than likely in preparation of this important Mandela Lecture, he crammed and did some research. Here is what he shared in his speech:

> And efforts like the Ouagadougou Partnership in West Africa are helping millions of women get access to contraceptives, which make it easier for them to care for their families.
> HIV/AIDS is another area where there's been good progress. Though it's a complicated story, and there are still big challenges ahead.

First of all he name drops by naming the Ougadougou Partnership. Did he donate to it? How long as he known about it? Did his foundation volunteer to lend perennial financial support? If any of this happened, he would have mentioned it. Instead, he simply mentions the work that is being done to let the audience know that he is "up to date" on what's taking place in Africa. Don't be fooled: these white boys have research departments and teams of interns that can do the research and write their speeches for them. The proof, as the saying goes, is in the pudding.

Secondly, he talks about AIDS and that there is "good progress" but that there are "big challenges ahead." How can there be both good progress ahead and big challenges. The big challenges trump any so-called "good progress" (redundant, by the way) that may have been made. In fact you really can't make the claim of "good progress" if at the same time big challenges are looming. In other words, Gates is a conglomeration of his own contradictions.

Gates continues:

> In a few days, I'll be speaking at the International AIDS Conference in Durban. When the global AIDS community last met there in 2000, only a few thousand Africans were receiving antiretroviral drugs. Today, more than 12 million Africans are on treatment, more than a quarter of them living here in South Africa.

So THIS is the reason why he mentioned AIDS! He's promoting yet another pontification-oriented speech. Just because more Africans are receiving drugs that are provided by the white man doesn't mean that there is progress being made. If a quarter of those getting the vaccinations are in South Africa, then share the progress with us. Just because you get a shot doesn't mean that progress is being made. What are the effects of the shots? Are there after-effects? What is the age range of the effects of the shots? How much are the shots? How many people can afford those shots without some kind of assistance? These are the issues that should be addressed and questions that should be shared with a South African audience, not how much dope the white man is injecting Africans with in the name of a "cure." Can you say Tuskegee Syphilis Experiment?

The praise from the financial "missionary" continues:

> So this is a huge achievement, and millions of lives have been saved. But the rate of new infections remains high. In sub-Saharan Africa, more than 2,000 young people under the age of 24 are infected every single day. The number of young people dying from HIV has increased fourfold since 1990. We need to get people to get diagnosed, we need people to seek treatment, and people who are on treatment need to be fully adherent.

How can he talk about lives having been saved when those lives were placed in jeopardy by the same people? White people and their intervention into the lives of people of color always brings heartache and death. These people do not enter into another culture's lives without using the art and science of imposition to take over that culture. They did it to the Mexican, the Native American and once the Asian came over here, they imposed it on them. They made the Natives go to boarding schools and forced assimilation on them. They enslaved black people and in the process waged a 300 year campaign of dehumanization. And the list goes on. In my view the health care approach, in the hands of the white man, is nothing but another form of militarism.

Gates continues to bloviate:

> Along with HIV, we have high rates of tuberculosis, including here in South Africa where TB/HIV co-infection continues to wage a devastating toll. So we need more creative ways to make testing and treatment accessible and easier to use. We need to get much more out of existing prevention methods like condoms, voluntary medical male circumcision, and oral anti-HIV medicine.

And herein lies what Dr. Frances Cress Welsing would refer to as "the keys to the colors." It is where Gates says, "we need more creative ways to make testing and treatment accessible and easier to use." When the white man begins talking about using "creative ways" to do something, those ways usually come at the expense of people of color. And when you hear the words "testing" and "treatment," just remember all those human experimentation activities that white folks still use behind closed doors in their hospitals, their "research centers" and even their prisons. It's all a part of controlling the people of the world who they fear and envy.

He adds another "idea" when he asserts, "And we're going to have to invent new and better preventative solutions like medicines you only have to take once a month or an effective vaccine." Medicine? The white man's medicine is what killed off tens of thousands of Indians in the name of a "cure." Read the history. Using a new medicine as the cover, he has waged medical genocide against red and black people for centuries. His newly established "community clinics" are often a front for his publication research. It's the same game, more modernized and intellectualized, but the outcome is the same: "oops! Sorry about that."

The pontification continues:

> If we don't act both on today's treatment and create these tools, the hard-earned gains made against HIV in sub-Saharan Africa over the last 15 years could actually be reversed. Because of the population growth, just doing what we are today is not enough. We need to do more.

By "we" is Gates referring to himself? He's the one with the billions of dollars that he claims to want to give away. So just put your money where your big mouth is and build, say, ten major hospitals and spread them all over Africa. That's what you call a plan. I'll even recommend the locations: as I see it, the headquarters should be centralized, located in the Democratic Republic of the Congo. The other nine hospitals would be located in Namibia, Angola, Mozambique, Nigeria, Sudan, Somalia, Mali, Liberia and Tunisia. This would be a major investment in the second largest continent on this planet. It would employ tens of thousands and bring immediate relief to the continent. What does Gates have to offer that can rival my plan?

Next we come to foodstuffs and nutrition. According to Gates,

> Nutrition is another critical area of focus for Africa. Nearly one-third of the continent's children suffer from malnutrition that stunts their growth and robs them of their physical and cognitive potential. Millions more suffer from micronutrient deficiencies. These are impacts that last a lifetime and impact whole generations of African youth.

Interestingly, black human beings were kidnapped from Africa because, in addition to their skin color, they were deemed better farmers than the Native Americans here on these shores. So on a continent with expert agriculturalists, you're going to tell me that there's a food shortage? The food shortage is because of white people's intervention and in a race war, one of the first things the French< Portugese and Spanish did was to take over and destroy the crops and the fields. Evidently Africa has not recovered.

And sending food from America is not an answer to what is taking place. The genetically engineered crops from the United States bring with them the same diseases that have infected the American population: diabetes, obesity, high blood pressure, various cancers and so on. Shipping those crops to Africa will lead to even more disease.

Remember those hospitals that I proposed earlier? As a key cog in those medical institutions would be major agricultural re-training courses and departments, run by African people, to teach the art and science of planting, field management and crop development to name but a few. These training programs would enable Africa to restore itself(hence, "RE-training) to what used to be and not rely on the white man's poison which will lead to the ailments that I mentioned earlier.

Now, pay close attention to the following claim and quote by Gates;

> African Development Bank President Akin Adesina put it best when he said recently that the greatest contributor to Africa's economic growth is not physical infrastructure, but gray matter infrastructure, people's brainpower. The best way to build that infrastructure includes proper nutrition.

African Development Bank? I had to look this up because as a Black Studies instructor I address issues of the Motherland as part and parcel of an understanding of the black past. When I learned about the existence of an African Development Bank, I knew something was amiss because I know that Africa's natural and human resources are depleting through immigration, death and general theft from outside sources, including China.

Let me tell you a few things. First, the way it describes itself as "a multilateral development finance institution." Do you know what this sounds like to me? A damn bank, that's what. And who can afford to take out loans, which is what banks specialize in? Not impoverished black people. So who is this "bank" helping to "develop"? Outside white interests who want to hunker down on the continent and open up shop, that's who. And in my view, that is one way to start a kleptocracy: faking and feigning financial concern while at the same time raping the people of their resources through "loan" programs.

This "bank" claims to have a membership of some 81 countries. There are only 54 countries on the African continent. The "bank" was formed on September

10, 1964, meaning that it has been in existence for 54 years. Here's the question: has the continent been uplifted during that time? Has the economic improved? Have civil wars and tribal conflicts decreased? The answer to all of the previous questions is "Hell no." So of what use has this "bank" that Gates refers to, been?

A bank takes in money, holds on to that money and then doles it out to "qualified" borrowers. This is a great way to start a kleptocracy. But in this way you don't have to steal the resources – you can have the gullible masses "entrust the resources" to you! Just as Africans and their descendants in the United States can be duped into accepting that religion crap (Christianity or Islam, same scam under different symbols), they can be led to "give us your money and we'll see to it that you get exactly what you deserve."

If there is a shortage of gray matter, then point your finger at the managers of this bank! If there are signs of poverty, point at this bank's priorities and ask where in the hell the money is going. And by the way, what kind of bank it is: is it a bank with any semblance of financial capital or it is more of a repository where rich whites from other nations can deposit and otherwise "hide" their revenue?

Gates further states that,

> Without eliminating malnutrition, we won't get the great potential that's there. We know that when mothers and infants get good nutrition, that breast feeding is a key part of that. We know that certain vitamins and minerals are essential for children.

So it comes down to the female and the child – the same two groups that the white man has successfully targeted right here in America. Gates' race has locked up the black men and left the black women in poverty to fend for themselves. Then he gives them coupons called WIC (Women Infants and Children) and tells them they can buy his milk and juices – all produced by white farmers, dairy owners and fruit growers, all having been contaminated by the white man's germicides and other "sprays." What goes in the woman goes into the child. And now we have ten year old girls with 36-inch breasts and 11-year old boys who are over six feet tall. It's called genetic engineering and the white man is an expert at it. And that's what he's going to do to Africa under the guise of being concerned about "nutrition" and "malnutrition."

Gates outlines an "intervention strategy" in the following paragraph:

> We have a number of ways to intervene to help nutrition, things like fortified cooking oil, sugar fortified with vitamin A, and sugar and flour enriched with iron, zinc, and vitamin B. One of the most exciting advances is the breeding of crops so they are naturally more nutritious. For example, when adolescents eat high-iron

pearl millet, their likelihood of iron deficiency is reduced six-fold. And just half a cup of biofortified orange sweet potato is all it takes to meet a child's daily vitamin A needs.

Of course, associated with the provision of crops, seed and outright food (dried milk, potatoes, rice, etc) are the drug provisions. Like the American food, the drugs that go through the white man's system, whether the company is located in the United States, Germany, France of elsewhere, are deadly and oftentimes have short-term value. "Breeding of crops" by the white man has the same end result as the production of drugs. As the saying teaches, "Short-term pleasure yields long-term pain." Gates suggests further that,

> The toll of micronutrient deficiency is huge, but the costs of fighting it are not. Recent estimates done in Nigeria and Uganda indicate that every dollar invested to reduce stunting returns $17 in greater earning capacity in the workplace.

If the costs of "fighting micro nutrient deficiency" are so high, here's an idea; have Gates take out a loan from that so-called African Development Bank, pay for the drugs, and the disperse them freely throughout the land! Gates can afford it and the Bank would benefit from the loan and the interest on the loan. Problem solved!

So far the Gates strategy is all about hypnosis and mind control: food, vitamins and other drugs and now we get to the actual brainwashing element of "the missionary syndrome":

> When children's bodies and brains are healthy, the next step is an education that helps them develop the knowledge and skills to become productive contributors to society. Improving education is hard work. I've learned this first hand through our foundation's efforts to create better learning outcomes for primary, secondary, and university students in the United States. But this hard work is incredibly important. A good education is the best lever we have for giving every young person a chance to make the most of their lives.

Of course white people know the importance of education because it is vital to their white supremacist system. Education is one of the first "opportunities" offered to the oppressed in order to condition them. They sent the Native American kids to "boarding schools" to be educated. They sent the African kids to white schools to learn how to assimilate. They took Spanish away from Latino kids and replaced it with "English only" curricula.

Show me a person of color who has been educated by white people and I'll show you someone who has been brainwashed. I believe it was the late, great Dr. Carter G. Woodson who once wrote that, "Before a negro can be educated by whites he must first be trained by Blacks." In other words, we need cultural preparation before we enter that white man's schools. But if the parents have been conditioned to believe that "education is the key," then they will in turn force the kids to go. In America the advent of Compulsory Education ensures that children of color will learn and internalize the "white" way of life.

Gates knows about all this, but frames it in a more descriptive and euphemistic way:

> In Africa, as in the United States, we need new thinking and new educational tools to make sure that a high-quality education is available to every child. In Uganda, young innovators at the NGO called Educate! are helping high schools prepare young people for the workplace by teaching students how to start their own business.

White folks always come up with concepts of "new thinking", "new educational approaches" and so on but they never change the system that is in charge of BOTH! What they offer are not changes in the old ways of thinking because many of those tenets must remain intact: such hard core realities as "niggas ain't shit," "the white man is right as usual" and "never argue with authority figures." Things like that. Now he may tweak everything else or add an educational nugget or two but the white man is not going to "change" in any major degree. He is too stuck in his ways, and those ways – which revolve around oppressing other people – have been quite lucrative to him. And after all, this IS a capitalist system.

Having successfully outlined ways to hoodwink Africans, now the white man moves to controlling their modes of communication – just like his ancestors did during enslavement. Check it out:

> And with the high level of mobile phone penetration in Africa, technology using mobile phones to connect to the Internet have the potential to help students build foundational skills while giving teachers better feedback and support. Globally, the educational technology sector is innovating and growing rapidly and it's exciting to see new models and tools emerging to meet the needs of educators and students who are not connected to current systems.

Cell phones – the bane of any civilization's existence. The minute they came into the culture, America began spiraling downward. If it's not kids continuing to contact one another even during school hours, it's millennials cursing each other out and setting up gang fights. Kids behind closed doors in their bedrooms unsupervised by parents setting up dates with old men and older women; adults on phones in their cars running into telephone poles and other drivers who are also on their phones. And it goes on and on.

As for the use of technology in education, the same doctrine holds: what goes in is what goes out. No matter how technologically advanced, the white man is always going to be a racist asshole. And therefore all technology allows him to do is to spew forth his intellectually racist and Eurocentric venom that much further and that much faster.

And higher education is not immune:

> At the university level, we need not only to broaden access, we have to also ensure that we have high-quality public universities that will launch the next generation of scientists, entrepreneurs, educators, and government leaders. South Africa is blessed with some of the best universities in Africa, like the one we're at today.

Being blessed with good universities and saving the continent are apparently two different things. Those universities existed when South Africa had a legal apartheid system – separation of the races – and those "scholars didn't do a damn thing. Those universities existed when Bantu education gave black kids an inferior quality of education than white kids and "coloureds" got, but the professors at those universities sat on their asses and collected paychecks. The universities existed when the Bureau of State Security murdered and harassed the black majority for decades and not a single "scholar" stood up against it. Fuck the universities of South Africa and the acquiescent assholes who serve in the administration of them.

Continuing:

> For our foundation, we partner with these universities to do our work in health and agricultural research. Maintaining the quality of this country's higher-education system, while expanding access to more students will not be easy, but it is critical to South Africa's future.

If this guy's "foundation" is so committed to helping, then just provide funding. That's all. Nobody wants white intervention on the continent when the track record of that particular race is taken into consideration. When white folks came to Africa, they had the Bible and we had the land; when they left, we had the Bible and they had the land. It's the same old neocolonial control that white folks shifted to as they modified traditional colonial rule and began using people who looked like the indigenous population to serve as their flunkies and control the masses of people.

Want proof? In this case the puppets are the South African leadership, which was modeled after the bootlicking that Mandela did once he got out of prison. Instead of kicking those white people in the ass for what they had done to his people, he launched some kind of "reconciliation" agreement and immediately went about the business of "taking bids" from the former colonial powers. Now, with him gone, the bootlickers that are left are busy doing whatever they need to do to get paid. Check it out as Gates claims,

> Other countries in the region will do well to follow South Africa's example and provide the highest-level university education to the largest number of qualified students. Healthy, educated young people are eager to make their way in the world. But Africa's youth must have economic opportunity to channel their energy into progress.

So Gates – the white dictator it seems – strongly recommends that other countries follow South Africa's example. In other words, notice that he (Gates) is dropping money into South Africa and therefore if the other countries want the same treatment, they'd better tow the line.

Gates further evangelizes, with an emphasis on the youth, that they must "have economic opportunity" to channel their energy into progress. This is a tactic that neocolonial control freaks place the most emphasis on: the gullibility and vulnerability of the youth. Wave money in their faces and call the end result "educational opportunity" and the young people's parents will make sure that their children "get the chance of a lifetime" and will ship them off anywhere so they can get an "edu-ma-cation." Then when they return they are as white-minded as any cracker you find on the streets of America.

The peckerwood puppeteer tells the crowd that, "Some of those youths will work in agriculture, where still over half of the workforce toils today. We need advances to make agriculture far more productive. Today, the seeds that are used are unproductive, the soils are not very good, and so many farmers grow just enough to feed their family." Notice that even when it comes to education, the issue of "food" is never far away. Control the food and you control the people who eat it. And since Gates has convinced these people that their seed is inferior, he will gladly steer them to the American form – filled with every pesticide, bacteria, and foreign substance you can find. And it will be reflected in the physical transformation that these Africans will undergo.

More "advice" from Gates on the issue of farming and harvesting, can be found in the following excerpt:

> With climate change leading to more severe weather, doing more of the same will not be good enough. The key to this is a series of innovation at every step along the way from farm to market. First, farmers need better tools to avoid disasters and grow surplus. Things like seeds that can tolerate drought, floods, pests, and disease; affordable fertilizers that have the right mix of nutrients to replenish the soil; and easy-to-administer livestock vaccines that can help prevent flocks and herds from being wiped out.

He is outlining needs that he knows will be met by white people. The white providers will charge an arm and a leg in the name of "assistance." They will sell the seed, the tools and the "education" needed to get the harvest from the farm to the market. They will sell the fertilizers which will of course be genetically tainted so that the plants can grow larger and in doing so, those chemicals will enter the blood streams of African people. Just as Americans are morbidly obese and riddled with diabetes and hypertension due to the farmer's greed, the same will happen on the continent of Africa. And along with all these diseases comes more assured control by the medical profession, quack doctors and drug companies to make sure that the people stay "doped up." Just like in the United States.

But the "dependency connection" doesn't stop there:

> Next, farmers need to be connected to a market where they can buy these inputs at a good price, and sell their surplus, and earn a profit that they can invest not only in their family's basic needs, but also back into the farm. This, in turn, will provide employment opportunities both on and off the farm as more prosperous farmers begin to support a range of agribusinesses like seed dealers, trucking companies, and processing plants.

This is how that which started off Africanized slowly but surely becomes whiter and increasingly Americanized. Who do you think is going to "connect" the Africans to the market? Who do you think is going to direct which markets are priority (white) and which are secondary (other than white)? Who is going to provide and monitor those "employment opportunities"? Who will own and control the seed dealers, the trucking companies and the processing plants?

The white man.

Gates and Warren Buffett are both pirates and profiteers, leeches and capitalists without conscience. But the difference is that Gates is younger and therefore more "on-hands." He gets right down there with the potential victims and works his dubious schemes on a more personal level. Case in point:

> I recently met with a group of young crop breeders, one from Ethiopia, one from Kenya, one from Nigeria, one from Uganda. I really love talking about the science of plant productivity. And in this case, I was amazed at the expertise all of these scientists brought to their work on cassava, a staple crop that provides more than one-third of the calories in many African diets. Some had ways of improving the nutritional content of cassava. Others were breeding a variety that can resist both of the devastating diseases that are threatening to wipe out the cassava crop.

There is something about what Gates just said that makes me think he was lying. First of all, he remembers the respective countries that each of the African scientists were from. Do you know how difficult it is for a white man to shed his "all niggas look alike" history and perspective and to actually care enough about black people to give them individual recognition?

Secondly, the idea that he admits that he loves talking about plant productivity. I'll be he does. Most colonizers know the importance of food stuffs to people all over the world. If you can control the food crop then you control the people who need that food to survive. Those scientists appear to be involved in "bolstering" the cassava and perhaps other crops as well. By bolster I'm talking about genetic engineering. What goes into that food is what comes out: when they inject those plants, that stuff goes directly into the human system. And as a result you have children growing far too fast, you have diseases like hypertension and diabetes on the rise and so on. Look at America; a bunch of fat kids and a rise in the number of people qualifying for disability because of diabetes related ailments.

Gates further notes that, "Our foundation is also working with a young computer scientist from Makerere University who designed a mobile phone app that lets farmers upload a picture of their cassava plants to find out whether it's infected or not." That is the façade that the young scientists will be duped into using (in exchange for a paycheck or a grant). They will dabble here and dabble there and the white man will tell them that they need to inject a little bit more of this or that and pretty soon you have a product that is marked "new and improved" when, in reality, is has a long-term negative impact on the African population.

Gates call these types of actions "innovators." Check it out:

> These are examples of the kind of innovators who can drive an agricultural transformation across the continent if they have the support they need. For many decades, agriculture has suffered from dramatic underinvestment. Many governments didn't see the link between their farmers and economic growth.

Nice terminology: "agricultural transformation across the continent." The only agricultural transformation across the continent that white people can take credit for was their kidnap of millions of African people from the continent and, in doing so, negatively impacted on the agricultural transformation that could have taken place if those African farmers and landowners would have been left alone! Innovators? There are more accurate descriptors, like "food manipulators," "genetic engineers" and of course the most accurate one of all, "land pirates"!
Continuing:

> Now, however, this misconception is gone. And through the Comprehensive African Agricultural Development Program, countries have a framework for transforming agriculture. The investment needs to follow so that young Africans have the means to create the thriving agriculture they envision.

The white man comes up with grandiose names and titles that serve to impress black people but really don't mean or account for a damn thing.
Break down the name, "Comprehensive African Agribultural Development Program. What's comprehensive about it? Does that mean that it includes all types of agricultural, all types of crops or all of Africa? How can it be a "comprehensive African agricultural" program when different parts of African have different climates and different soil development needs? And how can all of this be geared toward "transforming agriculture" when there is no real need to transfer agriculture, but the manner in which agricultural paradigms are approached and/or utilized? Any way you slice it, the poly-syllabic title means that "the white man (or an African English-trained lackey) is in charge. And that has ALWAYS spelled trouble for the African people. Look what they did to the American Indian when they (the white man) took control of all the land and therefore all the potential for growing corn (maize)!
Moving on to African agriculture:

> With Africa's farms as a base, the next step in economic growth is to promote job creation in other sectors. Doing this will require investment in infrastructure including energy. Seven in 10 Africans lack access to power, which makes it harder to do everything. Harder to get healthcare in a dark clinic. Harder to learn in school

when it's boiling hot. Harder to be productive when you can't use labor-saving machinery.

Gates seems to have it all planned out. Investing in infrastructure is first step in gaining control over the roads, streets, lights, sewers and other aspects of any city. After that comes the need for "code enforcement" which if course, will be written by the white man. Once you control the infrastructure and the code and zoning legislation, you can then justify the need for a "department" which, in all likelihood, will be headed by some white man. And you expand from there, linking that "Planning Department" with a "Finance Department," a "Department of Revenue," an "Economic Development Department" and of course some kind of legal department that ensures that if there is any resistance, it can be immediately squashed in the courts and through legislation written and enforced by, you guessed it: the white man.

Gates however, is smart enough to mask the strategy of "takeover." Check out what he says next:

> Ultimately, a shortage of power, like many African countries -- including South Africa -- have experienced, is also a drag on economic growth. Businesses will not invest fully in places where they can't operate efficiently. A recent report projected that 500 million Africans won't have electricity even in 2040. We need to change that.

When Gates says that "we" need to change that, he means "the white man must be allowed in and allowed to make the changes that are needed." Oh, he'll make changes alright; in the same way that he made changes to the Great Plains when he brought in the "iron horse" (the railroads) and used them to murder of First Nation people and the buffalo that those people relied upon for sustenance.

Yeah, he'll make "changes," alright. The same way he made changes when he traded baubles and beads for captured Africans and used those African bodies to create the most heinous system of enslavement ever known to human kind. With no electricity, the African continent will truly be "the Dark Continent" as the white man used to call it. Energy and the people who control it, is the capital for the future control of the world. As Gates put it,

> What Africa needs is what the whole world needs: An energy advance that provides cheap, clean energy for everyone. I've spent a lot of my time in the last two years working on this issue because it's such an important advance. I'm involved with a group of business people who are collaborating with governments to not

only increase energy R&D, but also to vastly increase the private investment in this area.

This one sentence spells out what Gates is about and what he is going to use as his means of control. He explains that, "I'm involved with a group of business people who are collaborating with governments to not only increase energy R&D, but also to vastly increase the private investment in this area." A group of business people – white folks. Not African business people but just plain business people. Without the racial designation it is clear Gates is talking about his fellow peckerwoods. This group of Gates' is "collaborating with government." More proof that they're white. What kind of "collaboration"? Not "cooperating" with government, but "collaborating, which has an entirely different meaning.

Gates knows the value and power of words. Words are tools. To "collaborate" with someone means, "work jointly on an activity, especially to produce or create something." This means that the government is also doing something with those "people" that Gates is working with. What do the government people bring to the table? What is their "cut" in the deal? The answer is that the government and these people will "increase energy research and development." A-hash! They will set ups shop, create a laboratory or science entity of some kind. They will be in charge and call the shots while the Africans sit back and watch. Gates and white folks will be calling the shots and doing who-knows-what in the name of "scientific advancement." This is how these white people intercede in the cultures of others: they bring in science or religion and use it to take over and otherwise dominate and direct the futures of those whose land and resources they plan to take control of.

Gates claims that the *collaboration* between white folks and their government pals have the goal of "increasing the private investment in this area." PRIVATE investment. Who will the investors be? Other white boys, which is why it is private. It will not be public, meaning that Africans can invest. It will become a monopoly run by Gates his white cronies and other white nations. In simple terms Gates is telling these Africans what he plans to do and how he plans to do it. This is not a pro-Africa plan; this is a pro-Anglo plan aimed at encroaching into and then hunkering down in Africa using the need for energy as their façade!

Then, perhaps realizing that he is exhibiting a little bit too much of the master plan, Gates is quick to sound empathetic when he claims, "I get angry when I see that Africa is suffering the worst effects of climate change, although Africans had almost nothing to do with causing this." What??? Oh NOW he wants to feel some sympathy and pity. NOW he wants to show empathy. Where was he at when those "worst effects of climate change" were materializing? He was sitting on his white ass with his wife biting into a filet mignon and sipping red wine in their mansion, that's what he was doing. Now that he's got his pencil-necked ass in Africa, he wants to sound like a techno-nerd version of Tarzan of the Apes!

Gates tells the throng, "The rich countries need to follow through on their commitment to double their energy R&D budgets so that we get the breakthroughs that are applicable globally, and we need to do that urgently." He's not prioritizing Africa: he's telling the so-called "developed nations' to join in and get a piece of the pie. He's laying out a business plan and vision for them to "come on over and get some of these African resources."

That's what "we get the breakthrough" translates to mean! Africans are in no position to join in on the "breakthrough," now are they? He's talking to European nations – Germany, Spain, Turkey, Austria, France, Italy, Scotland, Denmark and even the Czech Republic and Scotland! And his "plan" will be coordinated by all white nations and they will encroach on Africa just as they did during the colonial days and use "energy development" as their focus and fulcrum and perhaps pick up some diamonds, gold, silver oil and bauxite along the way.

Despite these facts, Gates exclaims the obvious when he declares, " Africa needs power now. And so there are many pragmatic steps we need to take even in advance of these new inventions." Since when did Bill Gates become an advocate for Africa? Where was he at when he was giving away all those computers and talking about donating all his money to white charities? He's speaking at an event named after an African leader who I think was questionable after he got out of prison (he served 27 years, endured the worst prison system in the world, but got out and found out his wife was getting some outside dick and couldn't take it – divorced her right away. What kind of "man" is that?), and now he (Gates) thinks he IS Mandela!

Continuing to talk down to and otherwise patronize the people in the audience (presumably majority Africans) Gates obviously never read his own words. Good thing for you that I did. For instance, check out the following slavemaster-sounding drivel:

> In parts of Africa, there's hydro and geothermal sources which are both reliable and renewable that can be exploited. There's been a lot of work on small-scale grids and the use of micro solar. This approach can provide individuals with electricity for basic purposes, but we also need large-scale power including well-managed electrical grids.

Notice that the geothermal and hydro sources are said to be "exploitable." Not utilized. Not used. Not applied. Exploited – which is a word that has numerous meanings in this context. Mainly, it means "to take advantage of," and that's what would have to be done. Those African countries that have the type of technology that Gates is talking about would be approached and asked to assist. They would charge a price. If the price is deemed to high by those doing the negotiating, they will simply TAKE it. This is how civil wars get started. Gates is starting to sound like a young Adolf Hitler.

Then he (using the term "we") goes for the gusto when he asserts, "This approach can provide individuals with electricity for basic purposes, but we also need large-scale power including well-managed electrical grids." So Gates is speaking macro=level activity - the big picture. He wants entire regions or better yet, the entire continent. And what's in it for him? Is he doing this because it will make him feel good? Is it his "Christian duty"? Of course not. This peckerwood is promoting a plan of global dependency that will further chain Africa to outside (white) interests. The bigger the land base, the more natural resources can be ripped off while using "energy development" as a façade.

In the end it's about money. They want to set up energy and electrical grids in impoverished areas. Gates says so himself:

> It means organizing the power system so that it's economic, so that the electronic bills are paid for, and so that the network is reliable 100 percent of the time. Once we get economic viability for these utilities, then it bootstraps the economy. It allows investments that are job creating.

Gates omitted the fact that before this process is "economic", it is first and foremost ideological. There is a philosophy behind the money that is to be made because all the main players – the proposal writers, the electricians, the energy experts, the developers and construction people – all of them are peckerwoods. The Africans will have menial positions, long titles and like their African-American counterparts in corporate America, will possess a bunch of keys that don't fit anything.

Moving on:

> So there are many challenges that I've laid out here: Challenges in health, education, agricultural productivity, energy, and creating enough job opportunities. These advances only happen in the context of governments that function well enough to enable them. I applaud initiatives like Mo Ibrahim's Annual Index of African

> Governments, which looks objectively at multiple measures of
> government performance in each country on the continent.

Such audacity? This four-eyed peckerwood talks about the "challenges that he's laid out." The challenges were there already. The challenges are all over the continent and were brought there by white incursions from various nations. The challenges are the white man's inability to accept the fact that black skin is superior to pale white skin which, by the way, can lead to various forms of melanoma or skin cancer. The challenges exist today in 2017 when wealthy white people like Bill Gates, who designs computers and related technology, has so much money he can think of nothing better to do with his time than to once again "invade" Africa and tell the black people there about the "challenges" that await them.

Gates tells the throng, "Citizens in other regions would be well served by this kind of comprehensive effort to spotlight and spread effective governance." In other words, "white power!" That's what this asshole is advocating; he's telling other would-be colonizers to use his model of infiltration, pacification and false contributions and then move on the land, the natural resources, and the latent and untapped talent human capital that is all over the continent. Of course there are so many sell-outs in Africa that he could also be talking to African "citizens" and telling them they can hoard the money and the riches under the guise of "development," but the key is to follow his (Gates') lead.

Gates' blueprint for oppression continues:

> A lot can be accomplished by focusing on fiscal governance and
> accountability. Here in South Africa, the government gets strong
> marks for the budget information it provides to the public.
> The International Budget Partnership, an independent monitoring
> organization, also ranks South Africa highly for its oversight of
> government spending.

Oversight of government spending? There's no telling what kind of deals Mandela cut with these white boys once he got out of prison. I knew he was going to be selling out when he forgave Botha and those white Boers for all those years of apartheid. Remember? Let me refresh your memory and remind you I was one of the people who fought apartheid in Nebraska as a student at the University of Nebraska Omaha, fought a donation of krugerrands to the same system, and worked with Senator Ernie Chambers to ensure that the state of Nebraska would be the first state to divest from that racist nation.

In other words, I don't just "talk the walk."

After spending 27 years in prison, following are some of the bullshit actions that Mandela took that endeared him to white folks (and coons) all over the world. As Gover (2014) points out in an article titled, "Nelson Mandela: Four Acts of Forgiveness that Showed South Africa Path away from Apartheid":

> **1. Mandela invites one of his former jailers to a dinner marking the 20th anniversary of his release from prison.** Christo Brand was a jailer responsible for guarding Nelson Mandela at Robben Island and then at Pollsmoor Prison. **2. Mandela invites his former prison guard to his inauguration ceremony as South Africa president.** Prisoner warder Paul Gregory and Mandela developed a bond during his long captivity … On becoming president of South Africa in 1994, he invited Gregory to the inauguration ceremony. **3. Mandela has lunch with the man who tried to have him killed.** Percy Yutar was the state prosecutor at the 1963 Rivonia treason trial at which Mandela was convicted of sabotage and sentenced to hard labour for life. Yutar demanded the death penalty for Mandela. Mandela said that Yutar had only been doing his job. **4. Mandela dons the Springbok rugby jersey at the 1995 rugby World Cup final.** During the apartheid era, few symbols summed up oppression for Mandela and his ANC colleagues than the hated green Springbok jersey. (Gover, 2014 – emphasis added).

The old song teaches us that, "The white man's heaven is the black man's hell." Look at the above: all that "forgiveness" to a race of people who were responsible for the murders of thousands of African people – men women and children. This sellout lasted 27 years, got out, kissed the white man's ass, but he couldn't "bear" the idea of his lovely wife getting some dick while he was locked up? What kind of psycho is Mandela? Did he expect Winnie to remain "chaste" or "faithful" while he was in prison for twenty-seven years?

Back to Gates' pontification-sounding speech:

> In some countries, individual citizens are leading the way. In Nigeria, 30-year-old Oluseun Onigbinde gave up a career in banking years ago to devote himself full time to pulling back the curtain on the Nigerian federal expenditure.

Take note that of all the countries he claimed as being locations where "citizens are leading the way," he mentions Nigeria. This pimp-like nation which seems to suffer a coup every year, doesn't even have free radio. Its oil is why the U.S. likes it so much, the the Nigerian people who come to America for education are some of the most reactionary and pro-white that I have ever met – and I've met a number of them.

The Nigerian that Gates singled out proves my point:

> With savvy use of data and social media, he founded BudgetIT Nigeria, which provides facts and figures the average Nigerian can understand. No doubt, he's a thorn in the side of some of Nigeria's elite, but to me he's an example of what one person can do to make a difference.

Nigerian elite? You mean the ones who have already successfully stolen and hoarded money from the masses? You mean the ones who are members of the military who use threats to take whatever they want? Gates doesn't know a damn thing about Nigerian politics just as he is lost when it comes to understanding black people in the United States. How can one person make a difference for an entire continent when years of upheaval, political change and billions of dollars haven't done it? Whoever this guy is that Gates has singled out (white folks love to single out black people as "the good ones"), he is more than likely an African Uncle Tom who curried favor with Gates (shined his shoes) and is therefore now deemed "a good spear chucker."

According to Gates,

> Governments have an opportunity not only to learn from what's been done in the past, but to do things in new ways. One of the exciting prospects is the role they can play in accelerating use of digital technology to leapfrog traditional models and costly infrastructure associated with banking and delivery of government services.

When you are talking about African countries, Gates has to learn that the African past prospered because white people weren't involved. Once the Europeans began invading the country, that is when the bad times set in and even now, with colonization having been minimized, that slick white man now comes around having re-named the white presence as, "new ways." They are not new; they are merely slicker, more covert and yet just as callous as the "old ways" of the white man, which basically means the use of bombs, bullets, and beast-like men.

One way that represents all three of these strategies is the advent of "communication technology." Gates says, "By using mobile phones, tens of millions of people are already storing money digitally and using their phones to make purchases as if they were debit cards." Storing money digitally? That has the white man's fingerprints all over it. First of all, the creation and then the sales of the phones. Then the bank accounts in which to "store money digitally." Finally, the computer system and technology to store and hold all those numbers and information. And then of course, the fact that the white man turns around and sells those numbers and related information to retail outlets and other sales entities because those numbers have become a part of a "contact list" or "mailing list." And the people with the phones are not even remotely aware of what is being done to them.

Moving on:

> A good example of this is M-PESA in Kenya. These services don't just give people a better way to move money around, they give people a place to save cash to fund a startup of a micro enterprise or pay a child's school fee. They create informal insurance networks of friends and families who can help with unexpected shocks. And they increase the profitability of small businesses by lowering transaction costs, making it easy to order products and supplies, and having greater security of financial assets.

This all sounds like a "system" to me and if you show me a system that is run and maintained by black people, I'll show you one that is inevitably CONTROLLED by peckerwoods. That what people like Gates do: they go around funding the secondary and tertiary dimensions of a system and then dupe black people into buying into it. All this takes place while the PRIMARY aspects of the system are under the control of white folks. They control the machines that make the parts, they control the parts and the distribution of the parts, they control all the data-related components of the system, the storage of the information and codes and location of those storage sites. So who really wins when all is said and done?

On a more pragmatic level, why would it benefit Gates to boast about or highlight what black people were doing? It would only be of benefit if he was working to convince people that black people were doing it when, in reality, white folks had the controls and the outcomes well in hand. That is what they do. That is even what they did with the civil rights movement in America; they made it look like King was in charge when, in reality, Rockefeller and some other rich white people met with King, A. Philip Randolph and for other "negro leaders," dubbed them "The Big Six" and then gave them $800,000 to split up. Their job became to get on the news and on television and "steer" the movement (translation: don't tear up any white property or talk about issues of race and don't join up with the Black Panthers or the Nation of Islam). Didn't know that did ya?

The point is that the person you see is not always the one calling the shots. And the inventions that people like Gates talk about are being talked about for a reason: it is because those in power (people like Gates) want to get your attention, win your trust and enlist you in a plan that will inevitably benefit THEIR system, not your much smaller needs and wants.

And yet Gates lays it on thick, never bothering to explain why what he is explaining in Africa isn't being shared with black communities in the ghettos of New York, Los Angeles, Chicago, Detroit or Philadelphia. Check it out:

> A digital financial connection can also help governments deliver services more efficiently. Studies from India show the government able to save tens of billions a year by connecting households to a digital payment system and automating all government payments.

Delivery of services by the government? That is one area where African countries have fallen way short. They may try and some have nonprofits that put in work in the smaller cities, villages and what we might call "hamlets," but there is no real service delivery system that can make a difference. The poverty rate is too pervasive, there is too much political instability and too much military greed and corruption. How can you save "tens of billions a year" when your Gross Domestic Product and Gross National Product is, at best, half a million? Automating government payments is a good idea but first you need to have enough capital and revenue generation to CREATE a payment system!

There is a difference between what programs WILL yield and what they CAN yield. In light of this basic fact, pay attention to the following claims by Gates:

> The early evidence suggests that similar programs in Africa can also yield substantial benefits. For example, recent research in Uganda showed that providing people with digital cash transfers rather than direct food subsidies not only saved the cost of delivery, it also improved nutrition because recipients used the money to purchase a greater diversity of foods and to space out meals as needed.

"Can" yield benefits, not "will" yield them. This is all imaginary bullshit, projected or anticipated results. There is nothing definitive. You have to have infrastructure in place and then a re-training of the population to be able to deal with the technological advances. What Gates is outlining is a pipe dream that is devoid of praxis and realistic application. Do you know what a "dream" is? It's defined as "hope without a plan." White people play into black people's dreams and then link any planning and all hopes to white presence, white resources, white assistance, white involvement and white leadership. It's what could be called "the new colonization strategy," and it is just as effective as the old, more brutal, forms.

Gates has defined what I see as a "Euro-institutional takeover" of the African continent. Even if blacks are in management positions, the white man, both on site and across the world, will remain in control. For instance, note the following:

> Governments can accelerate this digital transformation by implementing policies that encourage commercial investment, innovation, and healthy competition. Countries like Kenya, Tanzania, and Nigeria are already investing in the building blocks of this new digital financial platform. And I believe they'll see substantial positive returns. If there's one thing I'm sure of, it's this: Africa can achieve the future it aspires to.

Gates is forgetting a key point: before government can "implement" anything related to policy, the government must first of all be stable. It has to have a vision and it has to be able to resist taking money and stealing from its own citizens. African countries are notorious for their kleptocratic tendencies and that is what prevents them from "implementing" much of anything.

Secondly, the countries Gates mentions: Kenya, Tanzania and Nigeria are all countries rich in natural resources and are ass kissers of the United States on some level. There is an on-going college student exchange program going on and some of the biggest sellouts who are educated in American colleges hail from these three countries (and you can add South Africa and Ethiopia). Why else would Gates single out these three?

The key to white supremacy domination over Africa has rested on promoting divide-and-conquer and preventing unity among black people on all levels. And yet Gates has the gall to utter that, "The future depends on the people of Africa working together across economic and social strata and across national borders to lay a foundation so that Africa's young people have the opportunities they deserve." He's saying all the things that Malcolm X promoted, that the Pan-African Congress promoted and that all black nationalists advocated. But when we did it we were met with disdain-and-how-dare-you by Europeans in general and white America, in particular.

Now comes Gates mouthing "black unity" platitudes to a crowd of South Africans whose ass kissing former leader, Nelson Mandela, basically sold out the race to the same white Boers who had murdered thousands of people for decades.

Something is amiss. The African proverb teaches that, "It is a wise warrior who moves with caution and discretion when an enemy throws bouquets in his direction." And yet this throng of Africans, just like the coons in the United States, sits in utter silence listening to a white man talk down to them as if they were grade school children. Check it out for yourself:

> Recently, I had a meeting with students at Addis Ababa University. I started asking them the kinds of questions you would ask college students in the United States like, "What do you want to do after you graduate? What fields are you thinking of going into?" They looked at me like I was kind of crazy for asking those questions. Each of them had a plan for their future. They felt their parents had sacrificed for decades so they could go to this university. They weren't weighing their options, they had come to the university to get specific training, and they were eager to take that training and use it to make their country more prosperous.

Gates misses a key point: those students were meeting with him because of who he was. He was the founder and brains behind the most powerful computer company in the world. The reactions he saw were based on this fundamental fact.

Therefore when he asks them what they plan to do when they graduate, what fields they are thinking of going into – they see these questions as "set ups" that are asked to find out how badly they want to work – FOR HIM! The claim that they had a plan for their future is the kind of answer that these students have been programmed to give at an interview. Interviewers want independent thinkers and builders of companies because these are people who make good managers and know how to take orders. The fact that they believed their parents had "sacrificed for decades" is more evidence; they don't have time to start from scratch; here was Bill Gates and these kids came there, resumes in hand, willing to kowtow and kiss as much as possible to land a job. After all, before they can make their country prosperous, they have to fend for themselves and their families first, do they not?

Even with my logical explanation, Gates goes on to claim that, "They saw themselves as part of a large community with great needs. And they were going to dedicate themselves to serving that community by meeting those needs." How would he know how these kids "saw themselves"? He is sharing what HE (Gates) was hoping how they saw themselves! Rather than hiring all of these qualified young people, he can place the onus on them, instead.

Like most white liberal racists, the tendency is to believe that they know the natives better than the natives know themselves. This can be seen in Gates' following commentary:

> I see that sense of purpose when I come to Africa, and especially when I talk to young Africans. I think it's a unique asset that people see the need to change and that they want to give back. The students here believe not only in themselves, they also believe in their countries and the future of the continent. Our priority is to make sure they have the opportunity to turn those beliefs into action because young people with this sense of purpose can make the difference between stagnation and faster progress.

Can you see it? This white billionaire seems to KNOW the African; he can SENSE what they are thinking. Where did all this come from? Where has he been all this time? What did he do when South Africa was under the grotesque grip of the apartheid system? Why and how could he not see how Mandela had sold out his own people? Gates is part of a conspiracy of cultures, a global racist act that seeks to bind the richest nations together in a lily=white clique against nations of color, even as is being now between the United States, Israel, South Africa, the Soviet Union and a few stray white nations. Take notice that when these peckerwoods talk about the use of the A-bomb, it's never at their fellow whites (not even Russia, who they claim to despise). It's always brown people (Pakistan, Iraq, Iran, Venezuela) or yellow people (North Korea).

Knowing all this, when Gates says, "The students here believe not only in themselves, they also believe in their countries and the future of the continent", and then adds that, "Our priority is to make sure they have the opportunity to turn those beliefs into action because young people with this sense of purpose can make the difference between stagnation and faster progress," he is outlining what could be called a "buffer zone" or a "neocolonial system." White people use other persons of color to serve as middle ground managers to oppress the natives who are the real targets. That is who these young people listening to Gates will unwittingly represent while thinking that they are doing something for their respective countries.

Gates almost reveals his plot, but you have to be willing and able to read between the lines. According to Gates:

> Nelson Mandela said, "Young people are capable, when aroused, of bringing down the towers of oppression and raising the banners of freedom." But our duty is not merely to arouse, our duty is to invest in these young people, to put in place the basic building blocks so they can build the future.

Being "aroused" in order to bring down towers of oppression is what Mandela lost during his time in jail. When he got out he was in a state of what I would call "cultural malaise" that prompted him to forgive all his enemies, turn the government over to provocateurs, kiss the ass of oppressors, divorce his incredible wife, and curry favor with the white powers of the world such as Israel and the United States – both of whom invested heavily in the Apartheid system.

But arousing can prompt revolution and resistance. That's why Gates is quick to "correct" that word, He says that the duty "is not merely to arouse, but to invest." Do you see what he did here? He moved from ideological development and strategy straight to the financial and economic. In order to arouse young people you have to be a role model; in order to invest in them you have to have MONEY. And who has more money than anyone on the African continent at that moment? Bill Gates, that's who.

Gates is no revolutionary and he certainly does not want to "empower" black people. No white person does, despite their claims to the contrary. That is why Gates' next claim tells the throng that, "And our duty is to do it now because the innovations of tomorrow depend on the opportunities available to children today." The innovation of tomorrow? Do you think this billionaire white man is willing to turn the innovations of tomorrow over to black and brown people? The only way he would even consider that is if he had a group (system) of white people in total charge of every aspect of the innovations and the people of color would essentially be middle-management types. And those are the "opportunities" that this white man is talking about.

It's time to wind down this lengthy lecture, so Gates again raises the issue of "challenges":

> I'm sure it's clear to everyone that these are big and complicated challenges. But it's just as clear that people with bravery, energy, intellect, passion, and stamina can face big, complicated challenges and overcome them.

Now all of a sudden he talks in the third person. He doesn't tell the audience that THEY can meet the challenges and that THEY have the bravery, energy, intellect, passion and stamina that are needed. He says that there are "people" who need these things. If he was talking to the audience, why didn't he personalize the challenge? I'll tell you why: because the entire speech, as I stated earlier, is a blueprint for oppression and white supremacy and it aimed at those reading the speech from afar, not for the black and brown kids in that audience.

That's why.

Now with the hierarchy starting with the challenges and the people with the stamina, passion and intellect being on top (and outside of the audience he is speaking to), we then move down the ladder to a lower level on the tier and guess what we find? We find Gates explaining that, "There is so much more work to be done to create a future in which we can all live together, but there are also so many people who are eager to get to work."

Take note that Gates doesn't describe the conditions under which "we can all live together." That's a typical white tactics. They tell you what they envision as the future but forget to mention what your role in that future is going to be. Well, I'll tell you: it'll be the same. So when Gates says that "we can all live together," remember well that we all lived together during enslavement – only they had all the power, land and money and all we had were shacks out back and a 16 hour work day! For white folks that's about as close "together" as we're ever going to get!

Gates' closing words are these:

> Let's do everything within our power right now to help build the
> future that Nelson Mandela dreamed of and the future that we will
> achieve together.
> Thank you.

No, we can do better than Mandela's "dream." What did I share with you about a dream? It is "hope without a plan." That is what a dream is. And you see that King's "dream" never materialized despite that speech that white people pay homage to every single year. I remember a movie called "Attica" and one of the inmates told the camera man, "Don't nothin' come to a sleeper but a dream."

Gates is not asleep because he knows what he has done, is doing and plans to do. The people who are dreaming and sleeping are people of color who listen to this bullshit about philanthropy spewed forth by people like Bill Gates and Warren Buffett and believe that change is really going to come.

But it never does.

Conclusion

And so it goes. As I said in the introduction of this brief paper, Bill Gates and Warren Buffett are both capitalists, and the definition of capitalism is "the ceaseless pursuit of profit." And that's all either of these men cares about. Even when they claim to be giving money away it's more of an investment than it is a donation (the words of Warren Buffett). As you read my words you will see that Gates is committed to the same thing as all white billionaires: the maintenance of white supremacy and global imperialism with their race calling the shots. I have documented how he plans to use the African continent to achieve those ends using false benevolence and philanthropy.

Buffett, on the other hand, is more direct and could care less about a person of color unless it's someone he can take a photo with as he has done in recent years: Michael Jordan, Tiger Woods, Barack Obama.

These "new kleptocrats" really don't need military takeovers to steal from the masses. They can do so through policy, legislation and laws all aimed at "taking." This is already taking place in a number of local communities around the nation with cities and counties using "Eminent Domain" and various code enforcement strategies to take and relocate certain populations. And by "certain populations" I mean Blacks, Latinos, First Nation people and refugees. They can use fake evacuations, natural disasters as a cover for taking over entire areas and the media to circulate lies about gas leaks, electrical problems, prospective black outs and coming soon: the zombie apocalypse. A takeover is a takeover regardless of how it is accomplished.

The "new kleptocrats" will take huge chunks out of the American institutional arrangements and asset portfolio. Kleptocrats from Saudi Arabia buying up land in New York and parts of Michigan (even as Jews are passing laws to keep them from doing the same thing to Israel). Trump-like power mongers like Steve Mnuchin (CA.), Paul Manaford (CT), Ryan ZInke (MT), Wilbur Ross (FL), Rick Perry (TX), to name a few. You can see that their home states show how spread out they are. Will they ever attempt to forma conglomerate? That is now the "new kleptocrats" would begin.

Indeed, Trump is setting the stage by surrounding himself with family members, equally scurrilous people and those who are loyal to him and blind to his on-going atrocities. White people are slow on the uptake when it comes to seeing criminal intent when it is committed by their own people because they are too busy staring at what's going on in the ghetto, the barrio and on the reservation. But people like Warren Buffett and Bill Gates, smiling away, will introduce a new form of kleptocracy, akin to former President Richard Nixon's weird concept of "benign neglect."

The key for the "new kleptocrat" is the corporate entity that is global in scope. I have shown you in this book how both of these men have that element of kleptocracy well in hand. But the fact is, if you have a corporate entity that is using funds meant for development and you use that money for personal gain, what difference does it make it you're a "governmental entity" or not? *A kleptocrat is a thief and that is what is important.* The two white men I deal with in this book are not politicos (at least not directly), but they have a shared political belief: the belief in white nationalism and the token exploitation of black people to push their own causes.

That is the mentality of a slavemaster, or a dominative racist. Stripped of the smiles and the elderly gait, Buffett and Gates are white nationalists who use capitalism to amass wealth. It is not what they say, it is what they DO that should be analyzed.

References

Baker, Mike & Wagner, Daniel (January 13, 2016) Minorities exploited by Warren Buffett's mobile-home empire. Seattle Times.

Baker, Mike (2015, May 17). Buffett's mobile-home business has most to gain from deregulation plan. Seattle Times. Retrieved from http://www.seattletimes.com/business/real-estate/buffetts-mobile-home-business-has-most-to-gain-from-deregulation-plan/

Buffett, Mary & Clark, David (2011) *The Warren Buffett Stock Portfolio*. New York, New York: Charles A. Scribner and Sons.

BusinessDictionary.com. (2017). Retrieved from: http://www.businessdictionary.com/definition/monopoly.html

Clarridge, Emerson (2015). Cousins didn't mean to deceive Sherwood Foundation, Judge Rules, Dismissing Theft Charges. Omaha World Herald. Retrieved from http://www.omaha.com/news/crime/cousins-didn-t-mean-to-deceive-sherwood-foundation-judge-rules/article_eaa73c81-1cbf-58ea-bde4-7a983c554ad0.html

Cleary, P. (1979). The church and usury. New York, New York: Gordon Press Publishers.

Clifford, Catherine (2018, March 7). There are a record 2,208 billionaires in the world, according to Forbes' 2018 rich list. CNBC. Retrieved from https://www.cnbc.com/2018/03/07/forbes-there-are-a-record-2208-billionaires-in-the-world.html

Conlin, Michele & Smith, Grant. (2015, July 23). Trump university lawsuits damage presidential bid. Reuters. Retrieved from http://www.reuters.com/article/us-usa-election-trump-university/trump-university-lawsuits-may-damage-presidential-bid-idUSKCN0PX29520150723

Covert, James (2013, October 13). Buffett protégé caught in CEO sex mess. New York Post. Retrieved from http://nypost.com/2013/10/13/buffett-protege-caught-in-ceo-sex-mess/

Drake, Anne Caroline (2011, November 1). Doris Buffett: Giving It All Away (Book Review + More). Retrieved from: https://annecarolinedrake.com/author/annecarolinedrake/

Eyewitness to History (2001). "The Black Death, 1348," Retrieved from www.eyewitnesstohistory.com (2001

Gates, Bill (2016, July 17). The youngest continent: Giving the Mandela lecture. Gatesnotes. Retrieved from https://www.gatesnotes.com/Development/Nelson-Mandela-Annual-Lecture?WT.mc_id=07_18_2016_09_MandelaLecture_BG-LI_&WT.tsrc=BGLI

Gates, Bill. (1999) *Business at the Speed of Thought*. New York City, New York: Grand Central Publishing.

Goodell, Jeff (2014, March 13). Bill Gates: The Rolling Stone interview. Rolling Stone. Retrieved from http://www.rollingstone.com/culture/news/bill-gates-the-rolling-stone-interview-20140313

Gover, Dominic (2014, July 1). Nelson Mandela: Four Acts of Forgiveness that Showed South Africa Path away from Apartheid. International Business Times. Retrieved from http://www.ibtimes.co.uk/nelson-mandela-forgiveness-south-africa-apartheid-528153

Hagstrom, Robert G. (1997) *The Warren Buffett Way. Investment Strategies of the World's Greatest Investor*. Hoboken, New Jersey : John Wiley and Sons

Hall, Lena E. (2017). Paternalistic racism. Dictionary of multicultural psychology: Issues, terms and concepts. **DOI:** http://dx.doi.org/10.4135/9781452204437.n170

Karenga, Maulana (1967). *The quotable Karenga*. Los Angeles, California: Kawaida Publications.

Marketwatch.com. (2017, February 27). Warren Buffett Confesses Why He Sold His Wal-Mart Shares. Retrieved from http://www.marketwatch.com/story/warren-buffett-confesses-why-he-sold-his-wal-mart-shares-2017-02-27

Manes, Stephen & Andrews, Paul (1994) *How Microsoft's Mogul Reinvented an Industry and Made Himself the Richest Man in America.* New York City, New York: Touchstone

Mbembe, Achille, (2008, January 9) What is post colonial thinking? Eurozine. Retrieved from http://www.eurozine.com/articles/2008-01-09-mbembe-en.html

O'Loughlin, James (2004) *The Real Warren Buffett: Managing Capital, Leading People.* Boston, Massachusetts: Nicholas Brealey

Pearce, Fred (2010). *Peoplequake: Mass migration, ageing nations and the coming population crash.* Cornwall, United Kingdom: Eden Project Books.

Pfeifer, Sacha. (2016, August 13). Wanted: Help handing out Warren Buffett's fortune. *Boston Globe.* Retrieved from http://www.sunshinelady.org/?p=1370#more-1370

Robertson, Thomas (2012). *The Malthusian Moment: Global Population Growth and the Birth of American Environmentalism.* Rutgers University Press. ISBN 978-0-8135-5272-9

Schroeder, Alice (2009). *The Snowball: Warren Buffett and the Business of Life.* New York City, New York: Bantam Books.

Seventy-Five North Revitalization Corporation (2017). Retrieved from http://www.seventyfivenorth.org/about-75-north/

Starr, Barbara & Cohen, Zachary (2017, October 19). What we know and don't know about the deadly Niger attack. CNN. Retrieved from http://www.cnn.com/2017/10/18/politics/us-niger-investigation-what-we-know/index.html

Vegter, Onne (2017, August 1). Does apartheid still exist in South Africa today in some form? Quora. Retrieved from https://www.quora.com/

Welsing, Frances Cress (1991). The Cress theory of color-confrontation and racism (White supremacy): A psychogenetic theory and world outlook. In Frances Cress

Welsing (Ed.) *The Isis Papers: The Keys to the Colors,* Chicago, Illinois. Third World Press.

Winter, Greg (2002, May 19). Workers contend Coke sent old soda to poor neighborhoods. New York Times. Retrieved from http://www.nytimes.com/2002/05/19/us/workers-contend-coke-sent-old-soda-to-poor-neighborhoods.html?mcubz=3

Wong, Edward, Schmitt, Eric & Sullivan, Eileen (2018, October 11) Trump Calls Relations With Saudi Arabia 'Excellent,' While Congress Is Incensed. **New York Times**. Retrieved from https://www.nytimes.com/2018/10/11/us/politics/trump-jamal-khashoggi-turkey-saudi.html

Wood, Preston (2014, October 31). Ebola, imperialism and racism. *Liberation News*. Retrieved from https://www.liberationnews.org/ebola-africa-racism-and-imperialism/

Woodson, C.G. (1933) *Mis-Education of the Negro*. Trenton, New Jersey: Africa World Press.

WorldAtlas.com (2018) What is a kleptocracy? Retrieved from https://www.worldatlas.com/what-is-a-kleptocracy.html